wedding
readings,
poems
and vows

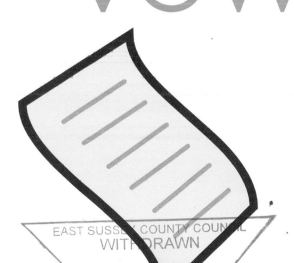

wedding
readings,
poems
and VOWS

hamlyn

confetti.co.uk

First published in Great Britain in 2007 by
Hamlyn, a division of Octopus Publishing Group Ltd
2–4 Heron Quays, London E14 4JP

Copyright © Octopus Publishing Group Ltd 2007
Text and artwork copyright © Confetti Network 2007
Readings and poems © Individual copyright holders

ISBN-13: 978-0-600-61645-0
ISBN-10: 0-600-61645-2

A CIP catalogue record for this book is available from the
British Library

Printed and bound in China

10 9 8 7 6 5 4 3 2

contents

Introduction

Readings at your ceremony can add an extra-special meaning to the day. Wedding readings are by no means a necessary or legal part of the ceremony, but they enhance it and allow thoughts and feelings to be expressed that are not explicit in the statutory words. Readings are also a great way to involve family and friends in the ceremony.

Church wedding or civil ceremony?

Whatever type of wedding you are having, this book provides individual sections on church weddings and civil ceremonies, which will explain the typical pattern for each ceremony, including what happens and when. All the readings in this book are equally suitable for blessings and civil partnerships.

Choosing your readings

The main part of the book selects the very best of love and marriage poetry, prose and Bible readings, divided into religious and civil ceremonies, as well as a chapter that includes readings suitable for receptions. Advice is also included on copyright, and printing your chosen readings in an order of service.

Writing your vows

The vows section guides you through the legalities of vows, providing a comprehensive guide to writing your own and also an inspirational selection of sample vows covering different situations. The vows are, naturally, the most important part of the whole day, and you'll probably want to spend some time ensuring that they reflect what you really want to say.

Even the standard wording will differ depending on whether you are having a religious or civil ceremony, or whether you have chosen an alternative such as a humanist, pagan or hand-fasting ceremony. Whereas some people are keen to follow the traditional age-old wording used by so many thousands of wedded couples over the centuries, others want to express something personal and individual, and put their own stamp on the proceedings. Whichever you prefer, you will find information and guidance in these pages.

Putting it all together

Throughout this book you'll find example readings, suggestions for additional readings you might like to consider and helpful ideas for putting together winning combinations of readings and poems.

For more ideas and resources, why not visit our website (www.confetti.co.uk). There you will find expert advice to help you select readings, poems and vows for your wedding.

Printing and copyright

When you have selected your ideal reading, check whether it is still in copyright. If it is, you cannot reproduce it (for instance, in an order of service) without obtaining permission from the copyright holder.

When it comes to the printing of the wedding stationery, many couples are concerned about the vexed issue of copyright. Most couples who marry in church will choose to have two or three hymns and a religious reading, and they will want to detail these for their guests in the order of service. Music for civil weddings may be more modern, but couples will still wish to provide details of each song and its author.

Copyright exists in creative works such as hymns, poems and prayers for 70 years after the death of the writer. During that period, it is illegal to reproduce the works in any form without the permission of the copyright holder (or their appointed agent). Should you wish to reproduce the text of a hymn still in copyright in your order of service, you will need the permission of the copyright holder, for which a charge of between £10 and £25 is usually made.

You will find the details of the copyright holder at the bottom of the page on which the hymn Is originally printed. But remember, many hymns are out of copyright because of their age and you do not need the copyright holder's permission if you are only singing the hymns, since a wedding is a private function.

Church weddings

The order of ceremony

A Christian wedding ceremony generally follows this pattern.

- Usually a hymn is sung once everyone is in church.
- A reading may follow, then the vicar (or minister/priest) states the reason for the gathering and asks if anyone knows why the marriage should not take place.
- Having received the couple's agreement to be married, the vicar asks who is giving the bride away.
- The bride's father, or escort, places her right hand in that of the vicar, who gives it to the groom.
- The marriage vows are taken first by the groom and then the bride, led by the vicar. After the couple have exchanged rings, the vicar pronounces them man and wife (although the full legal requirements are not actually met until the marriage register has been signed).
- Normally, the vicar will deliver a short sermon, one or two hymns are sung and prayers are said for the couple. Readings may also be appropriate here, before and after a hymn. At this point, the couple receive Holy Communion if they have chosen a communion service.
- The bride and groom, followed by the best man, chief bridesmaid, their parents, bridesmaids, pages and any other witnesses, proceed behind the vicar to the vestry to sign the register.
- At a given signal, the organist will strike up a piece of music and the party leaves the church.

Music and readings at the church

Music is played at certain times during a church ceremony. Organ music is usually played as the guests arrive and take their seats. The volume is raised as the organist starts to play the processional, which lets everyone know that the bride has arrived. Music will also be required to accompany hymns during the service, at the end of the service – when the couple are signing the register and, finally, for the recessional. For a religious ceremony, you are usually offered a selection of biblical readings, but you may also have the option of reading out a secular text. The readings or poems are usually given just after the sermon, with family members or friends reading a poem or prose chosen by the couple.

What are my options?

Biblical readings

Most services will include one or two readings. Ultimately, the choice of Bible text is yours, but you will probably want guidance and help, which clergy are always ready to provide.

Churches with a formal tradition of worship provide a choice of proposed texts. For Anglicans, the Alternative Service Book (ASB) carries a selection, and Roman Catholic couples are usually given a booklet with a fair-sized sample to choose from – although, again, you will usually be allowed to choose any text you wish from the Bible.

More informal churches, such as those of Baptists or Pentecostalists, may simply invite you to choose readings directly from the Bible, but will be happy to provide suggestions.

Secular readings

Exactly how secular the text can be will depend on the church in question, but perhaps also on the minister. A traditional high Anglican vicar, for instance, might allow some Shakespeare, but draw the line at modern poetry, whereas a 'trendy vicar' might be happy to consider a much wider selection of texts. Both, however, would want to ensure that the readings do not undermine the Christian view of marriage, so always make sure that your choice is checked and approved by the minister.

Choosing your theme

To help you decide on a suitable reading, it's a good idea to think about the sort of message you want your chosen words to convey. Although these can be surprisingly varied, three clear themes generally emerge:

- Marriage blessed by God
- Love is all you need
- Hints for a happy life

Marriage blessed by God

As you might expect, the most common readings chosen are texts from both Old and New Testaments that talk about marriage as being willed and blessed by God. Take, for instance, the passage from the creation story in Genesis, where God creates man:

'So God created man in his own image; in the image of God he created him; male and female he created them. God blessed them and said to them, "be fruitful and increase"....'

Genesis 1:27, New English Bible

Jesus himself quotes another passage to make clear his own belief in marriage as a lifelong commitment:

'Some Pharisees came to him to test him. They asked, "Is it lawful for a man to divorce his wife for any and every reason?"

"Haven't you read," he replied, "that at the beginning the Creator 'made them male and female,' and said, 'For this reason a man will leave his father and mother and be united to his wife, and the two will become one flesh'? So they are no longer two, but one. Therefore what God has joined together, let man not separate."

Matthew 19:3–6

Suggested readings: Marriage blessed by God
- The Beatitudes (see page 30)
- Creation of woman (see page 40)
- Two are better than one (see page 43)
- A good wife is more precious than jewels (see page 45)
- His steadfast love endures forever (see page 48)

Love is all you need

Other popular choices come from the wealth of texts that offer insight into the nature of love itself. Top of the pops here has long been the famous *Hymn to Love* from the first letter of Saint Paul to the Corinthians, chapter 13. Many will remember Tony Blair reading it at Princess Diana's funeral. Less well known, although equally uplifting, are various passages about love from Saint John's Gospel and his letters:

'Jesus said: "As the Father has loved me, so have I loved you. Now remain in my love. If you obey my commands, you will remain in my love, just as I have obeyed my Father's commands and remain in his love. I have told you this so that my joy may be in you and that your joy may be complete. My commandment is this: Love each other, as I have loved you. Greater love has no one than this, that he lay down his life for his friends."'

John 15:9–13

Some might object that the love in question is divine love and not the human, passionate love that is being celebrated in marriage. But if anyone suggests this, you can remind them that for believers, the point of the marriage ceremony is that human love is made holy and raised to the divine level.

And just to prove that God does not disapprove of human love, the Bible contains a whole book of passionate love poetry, the Song of Songs. It is rarely chosen, and by today's standards seems rather quaint, yet for the 5th century BC, its verses have an unashamedly erotic ring:

'Arise, my love, my fair one come away. O my dove, in the clefts of the rock, in the covert of the cliff, let me see your face, let me hear your voice; for your voice is sweet, and your face is comely... My beloved is mine and I am his... Set me as a seal upon your heart, as a seal upon your arm; for love is strong as death, jealousy is cruel as the grave. Its flashes are flashes of fire, a most vehement flame.

Many waters cannot quench love, neither can the floods drown it...'

Song of Songs 2:13–14, 16; 8:6–7

Suggested readings: Love is all you need
- Love (see page 32)
- Love one another as I have loved you (see page 35)
- My steadfast love will not depart from you (see page 44)
- Wives submit to your husbands, husbands love your wives (see page 33)
- Let love be genuine (see page 38)

Hints for a happy life

There is plenty of advice in the Bible about how to make your marriage a successful one, and no lack of texts on the moral obligations of marriage either. Of course, the ways in which biblical writers thought centuries ago may now seem rather outdated. Saint Paul, for instance, is often accused of male chauvinism and his advice to the early Christians of Ephesus seems to bear this out:

'Give way to one another in obedience to Christ. Wives should regard their husbands as they regard the Lord, since as Christ is head of the Church and saves the whole body, so is a husband the head of his wife; and as the Church submits to Christ, so should wives to their husbands, in everything.'
Ephesians 5:21–24

Modern commentators claim that what Saint Paul really meant is that husband and wife should give way to one another. Indeed Paul goes on to say that the husband 'must love his wife as he loves himself' and sacrifice himself for her. Although few feminists will be satisfied by this answer, a large number of women still choose this text, so some at least are convinced. Eastern Orthodox couples have no choice in the matter, as in their tradition it is one of the two obligatory texts in the marriage service.

If you are looking for something less contentious, however, try the following:

'You are God's chosen race, his saints; he loves you, and
you should be clothed in sincere compassion, in kindness
and humility, gentleness and patience. Bear with one
another; forgive each other as soon as a quarrel begins.
The Lord has forgiven you; now you must do the same.
Over all these clothes, to keep them together and
complete them, put on love. And may the peace of
Christ reign in your hearts, because it is for this that you
were called together as parts of one body. Always be
thankful.'

Colossians 3:12–15

So whatever you're looking for, the Bible is a
sufficiently vast resource for most people to find
something to suit them. Remember that your priest or
minister will be happy to help you, and if you're not very
religious yourselves, don't hesitate to ask family or friends
who may be more familiar with the book. Lastly, if you
decide on a text outside those suggested to you, stick with
the choice you are happiest with.

Suggested readings: Hints for a happy life
- A wise man builds his house upon a rock (see page 31)
- Wives submit to your husbands, husbands love your wives
  (see page 33)
- I am the vine and you are the branches (see page 34)
- The rainbow and God's covenant with Noah (see page 41)
- For everything there is a season (see page 42)

Music for a church wedding

A church wedding will include a mixture of hymns and other music. Most services have three hymns: two will begin and end the service and there is generally one in the middle, after the actual marriage ceremony. Some couples swap the middle hymn for another piece of music. Apart from the hymns, you will need to choose arrival or prelude music, as well as music for the processional and recessional.

There are many options with regards to the type of music you would like and also how it will be performed. Will you be using an organist, a choir, a soloist, or maybe a combination of these? Whatever you decide, make sure you discuss your requirements with the relevant people well before the wedding. They will probably be a helpful resource if you're having trouble deciding on music or are short of ideas. If you have musical family members or friends, this is a great way to involve them in the wedding. For example, you could replace the middle hymn with a soloist singing or an instrumental piece. It is details like this that will make your wedding service more personal and memorable.

Suggestions for church music

Prelude
- 'Nimrod', from Enigma Variations (Elgar)
- Ave Verum Corpus (Bach)
- Minuet (Boccherini)
- Sheep May Safely Graze (Bach)
- 'Air', from The Water Music (Handel)

Processional
- Trumpet Voluntary (Boyce)
- Wedding March from *The Marriage of Figaro* (Mozart)
- Hallelujah Chorus (Handel)
- Bridal Chorus from *Lohengrin* (Wagner)
- Grand March from *Aida* (Verdi)

Hymns
- Praise my soul, the King of heaven
- Jerusalem
- As I kneel before you
- How great Thou art
- The Lord's my Shepherd
- Lord of all hopefulness
- Morning has broken
- All things bright and beautiful
- Dear Lord and Father of mankind

Signing of the register
- Adagio in G minor (Albinoni)
- Ave Maria (Schubert)
- Ave Maria (Gounod)
- Panis Angelicus (Franck)
- Jesu, Joy of Man's Desiring (Bach)

Recessional
- Wedding March (Mendelssohn)
- March No. 4 from Pomp and Circumstance (Elgar)
- Arrival of the Queen of Sheba (Handel)
- Trumpet Voluntary (Jeremiah Clarke)
- Fanfare (Percy Whitlock)

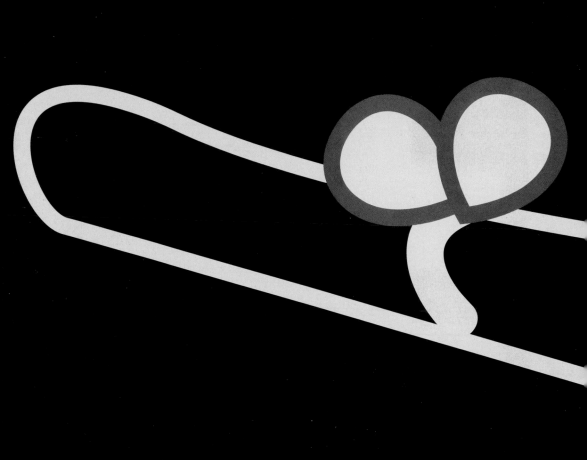

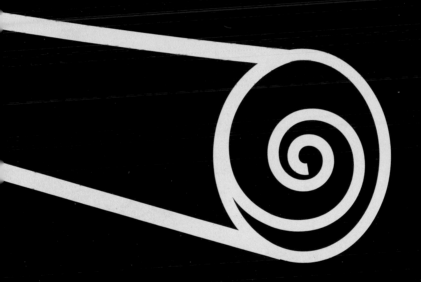

Bible
readings

Thoughts on choosing your reading

Choosing biblical readings can be both exciting and daunting, because of the sheer volume of passages. Although some pieces may leap into your head immediately and many more can be found here, it's a good idea to take some time to browse through whichever version of the Bible you prefer and think about which passages speak to you, and will speak to your guests. You can use the extracts in this book as a quick guide, then follow them up in your Bible or with your vicar/minister, enlarging or cutting the passage to suit the mood of your ceremony.

The listing of scripture readings in this book has been separated into three sections: the New Testament, the Old Testament and the Psalms. As with all readings and poems that you wish to include in your wedding service, you must discuss them with your vicar/minister first and obtain approval. You will also find some further suggestions for Bible readings at the end of each section of extracts, so don't worry – there are plenty of choices at your fingertips!

Chapter and verse

To help you find Bible quotations, a simple system known as 'chapter and verse' is used. Here's how it works. The Bible is divided into a series of books, contained in the Old and New Testaments. A biblical quotation is identified by the name of the book, often abbreviated (for example, Gen for Genesis, or Matt or Mt for the Gospel according to Saint Matthew). After the name of the book there are two numbers. The first represents the chapter number of that particular book, the second points to the verses referred to (these are the small numbers that divide the text inside each chapter). So, for instance, Gen 1:16 would mean the sixteenth verse of the first chapter of the book of Genesis. To help your search, you'll find a table at the front of your Bible giving the order of the books and their abbreviations.

Choosing your Bible version

It's not just a question of choosing your Bible reading. You can also choose a Bible version – that is, a translation. There are many available today, each with its own style, and some couples will have a distinct preference.

Lovers of English literature may well wish to hear the beautiful phrases of the King James version, dating back to the 17th century; while others may find its language hopelessly old-fashioned and even incomprehensible. Recent translations are more modern in their approach.

The Revised Standard Version (RSV), for example, sticks as closely as possible to the traditional translations, while rendering them in modern English. Others, such as the New English Bible (NEB) or the Good News Bible, try to be more up to date – sometimes at the risk of sounding banal. Unless otherwise stated, our readings are all taken from the New International Version.

The selection of readings given in the Anglican ASB is chosen from several versions, while Roman Catholics in general use the Jerusalem Bible, which is now available in an even more updated version using 'gender-inclusive language'. To give you an idea of what is at stake, compare these extracts from Saint Paul's famous passage on love; the first is from the King James version and the second is taken from the New English Bible.

King James version

'Charity suffereth long, and is kind; charity envieth not; charity vaunteth not itself, is not puffed up. Doth not behave itself unseemly, seeketh not her own, is not easily provoked, thinketh no evil; rejoiceth not in iniquity, but rejoiceth in the truth; beareth all things, believeth all things, hopeth all things, endureth all things.'

New English Bible

'Love is patient; love is kind and envies no one. Love is never boastful, nor conceited, nor rude; never selfish, nor quick to take offence. Love keeps no score of wrongs; does not gloat over other men's sins, but delights in the truth. There is nothing love cannot face; there is no limit to its faith, its hope, and its endurance.'

I Corinthians 13:4–7

New Testament readings

The Beatitudes

1 Now when he saw the crowds, he went up on a mountainside and sat down. His disciples came to him,

2 And he began to teach them, saying:

3 'Blessed are the poor in spirit, for theirs is the kingdom of heaven.

4 Blessed are those who mourn, for they will be comforted.

5 Blessed are the meek, for they will inherit the earth.

6 Blessed are those who hunger and thirst for righteousness, for they will be filled.

7 Blessed are the merciful, for they will be shown mercy.

8 Blessed are the pure in heart, for they will see God.

9 Blessed are the peacemakers, for they will be called sons of God.

10 Blessed are those who are persecuted because of righteousness, for theirs is the kingdom of heaven.'

Matthew 5:1–10

A wise man builds his house upon a rock

24 'Therefore everyone who hears these words of mine and puts them into practice is like a wise man who built his house on the rock.

25 The rain came down, the streams rose, and the winds blew and beat against that house; yet it did not fall, because it had its foundation on the rock.

26 But everyone who hears these words of mine and does not put them into practice is like a foolish man who built his house on sand.

27 The rain came down, the streams rose, and the winds blew and beat against that house, and it fell with a great crash.'

28 When Jesus had finished saying these things, the crowds were amazed at his teaching,

29 Because he taught as one who had authority, and not as their teachers of the law.

Matthew 7:24–29

Love

4 Love is patient, love is kind. It does not envy, it does not boast, it is not proud.

5 It is not rude, it is not self-seeking, it is not easily angered, it keeps no record of wrongs.

6 Love does not delight in evil but rejoices with the truth.

7 It always protects, always trusts, always hopes, always perseveres.

8 Love never fails. But where there are prophecies, they will cease; where there are tongues, they will be stilled; where there is knowledge, it will pass away.

9 For we know in part and we prophesy in part,

10 But when perfection comes, the imperfect disappears.

11 When I was a child, I talked like a child, I thought like a child, I reasoned like a child. When I became a man, I put childish ways behind me.

12 Now we see but a poor reflection as in a mirror; then we shall see face to face. Now I know in part; then I shall know fully, even as I am fully known.

13 And now these three remain: faith, hope and love. But the greatest of these is love.

1 Corinthians 13:4–13

Wives submit to your husbands, husbands love your wives

21 Submit to one another out of reverence for Christ.

22 Wives, submit to your husbands as to the Lord.

23 For the husband is the head of the wife as Christ is the head of the church, his body, of which he is the Saviour.

24 Now as the church submits to Christ, so also wives should submit to their husbands in everything.

25 Husbands, love your wives, just as Christ loved the church and gave himself up for her

26 To make her holy, cleansing her by the washing with water through the word,

27 And to present her to himself as a radiant church, without stain or wrinkle or any other blemish, but holy and blameless.

28 In this same way, husbands ought to love their wives as their own bodies. He who loves his wife loves himself.

29 After all, no one ever hated his own body, but he feeds and cares for it, just as Christ does the church –

30 For we are members of his body.

31 For this reason a man will leave his father and mother and be united to his wife, and the two will become one flesh.

32 This is a profound mystery – but I am talking about Christ and the church.

33 However, each one of you also must love his wife as he loves himself, and the wife must respect her husband.

Ephesians 5:21–33

I am the vine and you are the branches

1 I am the true vine, and my Father is the gardener.

2 He cuts off every branch in me that bears no fruit, while every branch that does bear fruit he prunes so that it will be even more fruitful.

3 You are already clean because of the word I have spoken to you.

4 Remain in me, and I will remain in you. No branch can bear fruit by itself; it must remain in the vine. Neither can you bear fruit unless you remain in me.

5 I am the vine; you are the branches. If a man remains in me and I in him, he will bear much fruit; apart from me you can do nothing.

6 If anyone does not remain in me, he is like a branch that is thrown away and withers; such branches are picked up, thrown in the fire and burned.

7 If you remain in me and my words remain in you, ask whatever you wish, and it will be given you.

8 This is to my Father's glory, that you bear much fruit, showing yourselves to be my disciples.

John 15:1–8

Love one another as I have loved you

9 As the Father has loved me, so have I loved you. Now remain in my love.

10 If you obey my commands, you will remain in my love, just as I have obeyed my Father's commands and remain in his love.

11 I have told you this so that my joy may be in you and that your joy may be complete.

12 My command is this: Love each other as I have loved you.

13 Greater love has no one than this, that he lay down his life for his friends.

14 You are my friends if you do what I command.

15 I no longer call you servants, because a servant does not know his master's business. Instead, I have called you friends, for everything that I learned from my Father I have made known to you.

16 You did not choose me, but I chose you and appointed you to go and bear fruit – fruit that will last. Then the Father will give you whatever you ask in my name.

17 This is my command: Love each other.

John 15:9–17

Put off falsehood

25 Therefore each of you must put off falsehood and speak truthfully to his neighbour, for we are all members of one body.
26 In your anger do not sin: Do not let the sun go down while you are still angry,
27 And do not give the devil a foothold.
28 He who has been stealing must steal no longer, but must work, doing something useful with his own hands, that he may have something to share with those in need.
29 Do not let any unwholesome talk come out of your mouths, but only what is helpful for building others up according to their needs, that it may benefit those who listen.
31 Get rid of all bitterness, rage and anger, brawling and slander, along with every form of malice.
32 Be kind and compassionate to one another, forgiving each other, just as in Christ God forgave you.

Ephesians 4:25–32

Salt of the earth

13 You are the salt of the earth. But if the salt loses its saltiness, how can it be made salty again? It is no longer good for anything, except to be thrown out and trampled by men.
14 You are the light of the world. A city on a hill cannot be hidden.

15 Neither do people light a lamp and put it under a bowl. Instead they put it on its stand, and it gives light to everyone in the house.
16 In the same way, let your light shine before men, that they may see your good deeds and praise your Father in heaven.

Matthew 5:13–16

Let love be genuine

9 Love must be sincere. Hate what is evil; cling to what is good.

10 Be devoted to one another in brotherly love. Honour one another above yourselves.

11 Never be lacking in zeal, but keep your spiritual fervour, serving the Lord.

12 Be joyful in hope, patient in affliction, faithful in prayer.

Romans 12:9–12

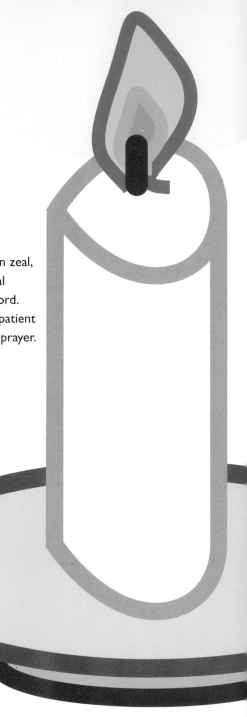

Other New Testament readings

Reference	Theme
Matthew 6:19–21	Where your treasure is, there will your heart be also
Matthew 22:36–40	The greatest commandment
Mark 10:6–9	What God has joined together let no man put asunder
John 2:1–12	Jesus's first miracle at the wedding in Cana
Ephesians 3:14–19	May you be grounded and rooted in love
Colossians 3:12–17	Put on love, which binds everything
1 John 4:7–8, 12	Beloved, let us love one another
Revelation 19:5–9	The marriage of the Lamb

Old Testament readings

Creation of woman

20 So the man gave names to all the livestock, the birds of the air and all the beasts of the field. But for Adam no suitable helper was found.

21 So the Lord God caused the man to fall into a deep sleep; and while he was sleeping, he took one of the man's ribs and closed up the place with flesh.

22 Then the Lord God made a woman from the rib he had taken out of the man, and he brought her to the man.

23 The man said, 'This is now bone of my bones and flesh of my flesh; she shall be called "woman", for she was taken out of man.'

24 For this reason a man will leave his father and mother and be united to his wife, and they will become one flesh.

Genesis 2:20–24

The rainbow and God's covenant with Noah

8 Then God said to Noah and to his sons with him:

9 'I now establish my covenant with you and with your descendants after you

10 And with every living creature that was with you – the birds, the livestock and all the wild animals, all those that came out of the ark with you – every living creature on earth.

11 I establish my covenant with you: Never again will all life be cut off by the waters of a flood; never again will there be a flood to destroy the earth.'

12 And God said, 'This is the sign of the covenant I am making between me and you and every living creature with you, a covenant for all generations to come:

13 I have set my rainbow in the clouds, and it will be the sign of the covenant between me and the earth.

14 Whenever I bring clouds over the earth and the rainbow appears in the clouds,

15 I will remember my covenant between me and you and all living creatures of every kind. Never again will the waters become a flood to destroy all life.

16 Whenever the rainbow appears in the clouds, I will see it and remember the everlasting covenant between God and all living creatures of every kind on the earth.'

17 So God said to Noah, 'This is the sign of the covenant I have established between me and all life on the earth.'

Genesis 9:8–17

For everything there is a season

1 There is a time for everything, and a season for every activity under heaven:

2 A time to be born and a time to die, a time to plant and a time to uproot,

3 A time to kill and a time to heal, a time to tear down and a time to build,

4 A time to weep and a time to laugh, a time to mourn and a time to dance,

5 A time to scatter stones and a time to gather them, a time to embrace and a time to refrain,

6 A time to search and a time to give up, a time to keep and a time to throw away,

7 A time to tear and a time to mend, a time to be silent and a time to speak,

8 A time to love and a time to hate, a time for war and a time for peace.

Ecclesiastes 3:1–8

Two are better than one

9 Two are better than one, because they have a good return for their work:

10 If one falls down, his friend can help him up. But pity the man who falls and has no one to help him up.

11 Also, if two lie down together, they will keep warm. But how can one keep warm alone?

12 Though one may be overpowered, two can defend themselves.

Ecclesiastes 4:9–12

My steadfast love will not depart from you

10 'Though the mountains be shaken and the hills be removed, yet my unfailing love for you will not be shaken nor my covenant of peace be removed,' says the Lord, who has compassion on you.

11 'O afflicted city, lashed by storms and not comforted, I will build you with stones of turquoise, your foundations with sapphires.

12 I will make your battlements of rubies, your gates of sparkling jewels, and all your walls of precious stones.

13 All your sons will be taught by the Lord, and great will be your children's peace.

14 In righteousness you will be established: Tyranny will be far from you; you will have nothing to fear. Terror will be far removed; it will not come near you.

Isaiah 54:10–14

A good wife is more precious than jewels

25 She is clothed with strength and dignity; she can laugh at the days to come.

26 She speaks with wisdom, and faithful instruction is on her tongue.

27 She watches over the affairs of her household and does not eat the bread of idleness.

28 Her children arise and call her blessed; her husband also, and he praises her:

29 'Many women do noble things, but you surpass them all.'

30 Charm is deceptive, and beauty is fleeting; but a woman who fears the Lord is to be praised.

31 Give her the reward she has earned, and let her works bring her praise at the city gate.

Proverbs 31:25–31

Other Old Testament readings

Reference	Theme
Joshua 24:15	As for me and my house, we will serve the Lord
Ruth 1:16–17	Whither thou goest I will go
Proverbs 3:1–6, 13–18	Let not loyalty and faithfulness forsake you
Isaiah 30:21	This is the way, walk in it
Isaiah 32:2,16–18	Each will be like a hiding place, like streams in dry land
Isaiah 61:10–11	Clothed in salvation... as a bride adorns herself with her jewels
Jeremiah 33:10–11	There will be heard once more the voices of the bride and bridegroom
Hosea 2:19–20	I will betroth you to me for ever

Psalms

Let us sing to the Lord

1 Come, let us sing for joy to the Lord; let us shout aloud to the Rock of our salvation.

2 Let us come before him with thanksgiving and extol him with music and song.

3 For the Lord is the great God, the great King above all gods.

4 In his hand are the depths of the earth, and the mountain peaks belong to him.

5 The sea is his, for he made it, and his hands formed the dry land.

6 Come, let us bow down in worship, let us kneel before the Lord our Maker;

7 for he is our God and we are the people of his pasture, the flock under his care.

Let us sing to the Lord.

Psalm 95:1–7

His steadfast love endures forever

1 Give thanks to the Lord, for he is good. His love endures for ever.

2 Give thanks to the God of gods. His love endures for ever.

3 Give thanks to the Lord of lords: His love endures for ever;

4 To him who alone does great wonders, His love endures for ever;

5 Who by his understanding made the heavens, His love endures for ever;

6 Who spread out the earth upon the waters, His love endures for ever;

7 Who made the great lights – His love endures for ever;

8 The sun to govern the day, His love endures for ever;

9 The moon and stars to govern the night; His love endures for ever.

Psalm 136:1–9

Other Psalms

Reference	Theme
Psalm 8	O Lord, how majestic is thy name
Psalm 34: 1-3	Let us exalt his name together
Psalm 67	May God be gracious to us and bless us
Psalm 100	Make a joyful noise to the Lord
Psalm 121	He will watch over your going out and your coming in
Psalm 127	Unless the Lord builds the house
Psalm 128	May you see your children's children
Psalm 150	Praise the Lord!

Prayers

Father, as we celebrate the marriage of ___ and ___, strengthen our love for those close to us; let us share the wonder of creation out of your love, and your presence in our world. Allow ___ and ___ to enjoy the commitment they have made to each other and grant us happiness as we share in their joy. Amen.

Eternal God, as we share in this joyful occasion, Bless us and ___ and ___ as we pray that they will love and care for each other for the rest of their lives. Bless this wedding and the gifts of love and happiness it brings to us all. Amen.

God of love, creator of heaven and earth, we praise you for your love and strength, and for the wonderful gift of marriage.

We pray for ___ and ___, for their love for each other, and for all the joy brought through the alliance of marriage.

We thank you for your love and commitment, and we thank you for your guidance of ___ and ___ through their preparation for marriage.

Lord God, help ___ and ___ to be loyal
and faithful, let them support each other
through life.

Let them share their joys and burdens,
and help them to honour the vows
that they have made to each
other today.

Help them to be wise in
their decisions, honest
with each other, and kind
and loving to the people
who support them.

Help ___ and ___ to grow
strong together, and let
them enjoy the experience
of love for ever until their
lives shall end. Amen.

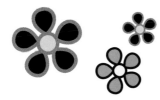

Our Father, may your love strengthen and support us, and your wisdom deepen our knowledge.

Let your love guide us in our everyday lives as we take on new challenges, through Jesus Christ our Lord. Amen.

God of love, we pray for ___ and ___ on this day as they make the commitment of marriage on this joyful occasion.

Guide them through their decisions and support them in their choices. Bless their children and allow them to enjoy your blessing and serve your world. Amen.

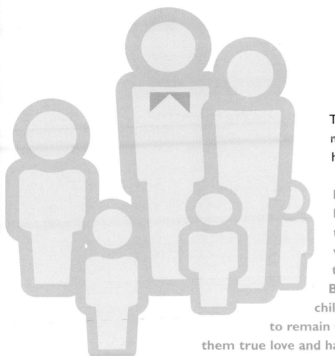

This prayer is suitable for second marriages and for those who have children.

Father, we thank you for your blessing of this family, allowing these parents to share new joy with one another. We pray for them to enjoy a happy life. Bless their children and their children's children, and help them to remain true to one another. Grant them true love and happiness for ever more. Amen.

To be said by the couple:
God of love and strength, we thank you for your blessing today, and for your guidance that has led our paths to cross.

Guide us in our decisions through our marriage, in good, bad, stability and change.

Help us to support each other and be worthy of each other, and protect and care for us and our home.

We trust and believe in you, now and for ever, for the rest of our lives, through Jesus Christ our Lord. Amen.

Readings for a
church
ceremony

Choosing your readings

Readings aren't necessarily just for the ceremony. If you can't decide between readings, or don't want to include them in your wedding service, you could consider having them at the reception. A reading before the wedding breakfast or to introduce the speeches makes a great personal touch. There are also some beautiful readings that are suitable to be spoken by the couple who have just married, or for other members of the family, and we've included a selection of these here. When you have selected your ideal reading, check whether it is still in copyright. If it is, you cannot reproduce it (for instance, in an order of service) without obtaining permission from the copyright holder. See pages 8–9 for more details on this.

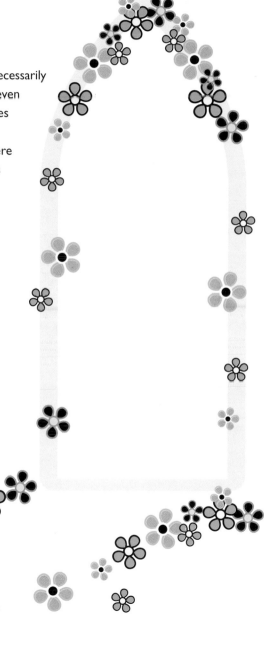

The readings given in this book are not necessarily limited to those of the Anglican Church or even the Christian tradition. Our selection includes many readings that celebrate all aspects of spirituality and love. The pieces suggested here represent some of the most enduring pieces of romantic poetry and prose ever written, with sentiments as valid and meaningful to couples now as they have been over many hundreds of years. The writings of Dante from the 13th century and the words of 14th-century poet Thomas à Kempis still encapsulate many couples' thoughts and emotions about their union.

Never Marry but for Love

William Penn (1644–1718)

Never marry but for love; but see that thou lovest what is lovely. He that minds a body and not a soul has not the better part of that relationship, and will consequently lack the noblest comfort of a married life.

Between a man and his wife nothing ought to rule but love. As love ought to bring them together, so it is the best way to keep them well together.

A husband and wife that love one another show their children that they should do so too. Others visibly lose their authority in their families by their contempt of one another, and teach their children to be unnatural by their own examples.

Let not enjoyment lessen, but augment, affection; it being the basest of passions to like when we have not, what we slight when we possess.

Here it is we ought to search out our pleasure, where the field is large and full of variety, and of an enduring nature; sickness, poverty or disgrace being not able to shake it because it is not under the moving influences of worldly contingencies.

Nothing can be more entire and without reserve; nothing more zealous, affectionate and sincere; nothing more contented than such a couple, nor greater temporal felicity than to be one of them.

The Newly-Wedded
Winthrop Mackworth Praed (1802–1839)

More like this

Captain Correlli's Mandolin, Chapter 47
Louis de Bernières

Lullaby
WH Auden

Now the rite is duly done;
Now the word is spoken;
And the spell has made us one
Which may ne'er be broken:
Rest we, dearest, in our home, –
Roam we o'er the heather, –
We shall rest, and we shall roam,
Shall we not? together.

From this hour the summer rose
Sweeter breathes to charm us;
From this hour the winter snows
Lighter fall to harm us:
Fair or foul – on land or sea –
Come the wind or weather,
Best and worst, whate'er they be,
We shall share together.

Death, who friend from friend can part,
Brother rend from brother,
Shall but link us, heart and heart,
Closer to each other:
We will call his anger play,
Deem his dart a feather,
When we meet him on our way
Hand in hand together.

To Celia

Ben Jonson (1572–1637)

Drink to me only with thine eyes,
And I will pledge with mine;
Or leave a kisse but in the cup,
And I'll not look for wine.
The thirst that from the soul doth rise,
Doth ask a drink divine;
But might I of Jove's nectar sup,
I would not change for thine.
I sent thee late a rosie wreath,
Not so much honouring thee,
As giving it a hope, that there
It could not withered bee.
But thou thereon didst only breathe,
And sent'st it back to me;
Since when it grows, and smells, I swear,
Not of itself, but thee.

Love's Philosophy

Percy Bysshe Shelley (1792–1822)

The fountains mingle with the river
And the rivers with the oceans,
The winds of heaven mix forever
With a sweet emotion;
Nothing in the world is single;
All things by a law divine
In one spirit meet and mingle.
Why not I with thine?

Winning combinations

I Corinthians 13:4–13
(see page 32)

Ephesians 5:21–33
(see page 33)

See the mountains kiss high heaven
And the waves clasp one another;
No sister-flower would be forgiven
If it disdained its brother,
And the sunlight clasps the earth
And the moonbeams kiss the sea:
What is all this sweet work worth
If thou kiss not me?

No. 43 from *Sonnets from the Portuguese*
Elizabeth Barrett Browning (1806–1861)

How do I love thee? Let me count the ways.
I love thee to the depth and breadth and height
My soul can reach, when feeling out of sight
For the ends of Being and ideal Grace.
I love thee to the level of every day's
Most quiet need, by sun and candle light.
I love thee freely, as men strive for Right;
I love thee purely, as they turn from Praise.
I love thee with the passion put to use
In my old griefs, and with my
childhood's faith.

I love thee with a love I seemed to lose
With my lost saints, – I love thee
with the breath,
Smiles, tears, of all my life! –
and, if God choose,
I shall but love thee better
after death.

Extract from *De Imitatio Christi*

Thomas à Kempis (1379–1471)

Love is a mighty power, a great and complete good.
Love alone lightens every burden, and makes rough places
smooth.
It bears every hardship as though it were nothing, and
renders all bitterness sweet and acceptable.

Nothing is sweeter than love,
Nothing stronger,
Nothing higher,
Nothing wider,
Nothing more pleasant,
Nothing fuller or better in heaven or earth; for love is
born of God.

Love flies, runs and leaps for joy.
It is free and unrestrained.
Love knows no limits, but ardently transcends all bounds.
Love feels no burden, takes no account of toil,
Attempts things beyond its strength.

Perfect Woman

William Wordsworth (1770–1850)

She was a phantom of delight
When first she gleam'd upon my sight;
A lovely apparition, sent
To be a moment's ornament;
Her eyes as stars of twilight fair;
Like twilight's, too, her dusky hair;
But all things else about her drawn
From May-time and the cheerful dawn;
A dancing shape, an image gay,
To haunt, to startle, and waylay.
I saw her upon nearer view,
A Spirit, yet a Woman too!
Her household motions light and free,
And steps of virgin liberty;
A countenance in which did meet

Sweet records, promises as sweet:
A creature not too bright or good
For human nature's daily food;
For transient sorrows, simple wiles,
Praise, blame, love, kisses, tears and smiles.
And now I see with eye serene
The very pulse of the machine;
A being breathing thoughtful breath,
A traveller between life and death;
The reason firm, the temperate will,
Endurance, foresight, strength, and skill;
A perfect Woman, nobly plann'd,
To warn, to comfort, and command;
And yet a Spirit still, and bright
With something of angelic light.

To My Dear and Loving Husband

Anne Bradstreet (c.1612–1672)

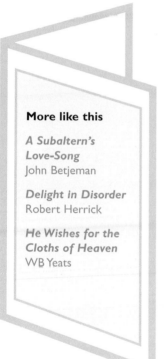

More like this

*A Subaltern's
Love-Song*
John Betjeman

Delight in Disorder
Robert Herrick

*He Wishes for the
Cloths of Heaven*
WB Yeats

If ever two were one, then surely we.
If ever man were lov'd by wife, then thee.
If ever wife was happy in a man,
Compare with me, ye women, if you can.
I prize thy love more than whole Mines of gold
Or all the riches that the East doth hold.
My love is such that Rivers cannot quench,
Nor ought but love from thee give recompense.
Thy love is such I can no way repay.
The heavens reward thee manifold, I pray.
Then while we live, in love let's so persevere
That when we live no more, we may live ever.

Love Lives

John Clare (1793–1864)

Love lives beyond
The tomb, the earth, which fades like dew.
I love the fond,
The faithful, and the true

Love lives in sleep,
The happiness of healthy dreams
Eve's dews may weep,
But love delightful seems.

'Tis heard in Spring
When light and sunbeams, warm and kind,
On angels' wing
Bring love and music to the mind.

And where is voice,
So young, so beautiful and sweet
As nature's choice,
Where Spring and lovers meet?

Love lives beyond
The tomb, the earth, the flowers, and dew.
I love the fond,
The faithful, young and true.

One Day I Wrote Her Name Upon the Strand

Edmund Spenser (1552–1599)

Winning combinations

Genesis 2:20–24
(see page 40)

Ecclesiastes 4:9–12
(see page 43)

One day I wrote her name upon the strand,
But came the waves and washed it away:
Again I wrote it with a second hand,
But came the tide, and made my pains his prey.
Vain man, said she, that dost in vain assay
A mortal thing so to immortalize!
For I myself shall like to this decay,
And eke my name be wiped out likewise.
Not so (quoth I), let baser things devise
To die in dust, but you shall live by fame:
My verse your virtues rare shall eternize,
And in the heavens write your glorious name:
Where, whereas Death shall all the world subdue,
Our love shall live, and later life renew.

Destiny
Sir Edwin Arnold (1832–1904)

Somewhere there waiteth in this world of ours
For one lone soul another lonely soul,
Each choosing each through all the weary hours
And meeting strangely at one sudden goal.
Then blend they, like green leaves with golden flowers,
Into one beautiful and perfect whole;
And life's long night is ended, and the way
Lies open onward to eternal day.

Extract from *The Divine Comedy*
Dante (1265–1321)

The love of God, unutterable and perfect, flows into a pure
soul the way light rushes into a transparent object. The more
love we receive, the more love we shine forth; so that, as
we grow clear and open, the more complete the joy of loving
is. And the more souls who resonate together, the greater
the intensity of their love for, mirror-like, each soul reflects
the other.

Friendship
Hartley Coleridge (1796–1849)

More like this

To the Virgins, To Make Much of Time
Robert Herrick

The Confirmation
Edwin Muir

When we were idlers with the loitering rills,
The need of human love we little noted:
Our love was nature; and the peace that floated
On the white mist,
And dwelt upon the hills,
To sweet accord subdued our wayward wills:
One soul was ours, one mind, one heart devoted,
That, wisely doting, ask'd not why it doted,
And ours the unknown joy, which knowing kills.
But now I find how dear thou wert to me;
That man is more than half of nature's treasure,
Of that fair beauty which no eye can see,
Of that sweet music which no ear can measure;
And now the streams may sing for others' pleasure,
The hills sleep on in their eternity.

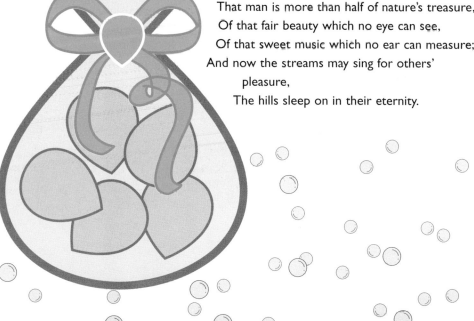

True Woman – Her Love
Dante Gabriel Rossetti (1828–1882)

She loves him; for her infinite soul is Love,
And he her lode-star. Passion in her is
A glass facing his fire, where the bright bliss
Is mirrored, and the heat returned. Yet move
    That glass, a stranger's amorous flame to prove,
      And it shall turn, by instant contraries,
        Ice to the moon; while her pure fire to his
          For whom it burns, clings close i' the heart's alcove.

    Lo! they are one. With wifely breast to breast
    And circling arms, she welcomes all command
Of love, – her soul to answering ardours fann'd:
Yet as morn springs or twilight sinks to rest,
    Ah! who shall say she deems not loveliest
      The hour of sisterly sweet hand-in-hand?

My Delight and Thy Delight

Robert Bridges (1844–1930)

My delight and thy delight
Walking, like two angels white,
In the gardens of the night:

My desire and thy desire
Twining to a tongue of fire,
Leaping live, and laughing higher:

Thro' the everlasting strife
In the mysteries of life.
Love, from whom the world begun,
Hath the secret of the sun.

Love can tell, and love alone,
Whence the million stars were strewn,
Why each atom knows its own,
How, in spite of woe and death,
Gay is life, and sweet is breath:

This he taught us, this we knew,
Happy in his science true,
Hand in hand as we stood
'Neath the shadows of the wood,
Heart to heart as we lay
In the dawning of the day.

Extracts from *Romeo and Juliet*
William Shakespeare (1564–1616)

Winning combinations

Matthew 7:24–29
(see page 31)

Proverbs 31:25–31
(see page 45)

Love is a smoke made with the fume of sighs;
Being purg'd, a fire sparkling in lovers' eyes;
Being vex'd, a sea nourish'd with lovers' tears;
What is it else? A madness most discreet,
A choking gall, and a preserving sweet.
Act I.I

O, she doth teach the torches to burn bright!
Her beauty hangs upon the cheek of night
Like a rich jewel in an Ethiop's ear;
Beauty too rich for use, for earth too dear!
So shows a snowy dove trooping with crows,
As yonder lady o'er her fellows shows.
The measure done, I'll watch her place of stand,
And, touching hers, make blessed my rude hand.
Did my heart love till now? Forswear it, sight!
For I ne'er saw true beauty till this night.
Act I.V

But soft! What light through yonder window breaks?
It is the East and Juliet is the sun!
Arise, fair sun, and kill the envious moon,
Who is already sick and pale with grief
That thou her maid art more fair than she.
Be not her maid, since she is envious.
Her vestal livery is but sick and green,
And none but fools do wear it. Cast it off.
It is my lady; O it is my love!
O that she knew she were!
She speaks, yet she says nothing. What of that?
Her eye discourses; I will answer it.
I am too bold; 'tis not to me she speaks.
Two of the fairest stars in all the heaven,
Having some business, do entreat her eyes
To twinkle in their spheres till they return.
What if her eyes were there, they in her head?
The brightness of her cheek would shame those stars
As daylight doth a lamp; her eyes in heaven
Would through the airy region stream so bright
That birds would sing and think it were not night.
See how she leans her cheek upon her hand!
O that I were a glove upon that hand,
That I might touch that cheek!

Act II.II

Extract from *Twelfth Night*
William Shakespeare (1564–1616)

Oh mistress mine! where are you roaming?
O, stay and hear; your true love's coming.
That can sing both high and low.
Trip no further, pretty sweeting;
Journeys end in lovers meeting,
Every wise man's son doth know.

What is love? 'tis not hereafter;
Present mirth hath present laughter;
What's to come is still unsure;
In delay there lies no plenty;
Then come kiss me, sweet and twenty,
Youth's a stuff will not endure.
Act II.III

Sonnet 18
William Shakespeare (1564–1616)

Shall I compare thee to a summer's day?
Thou art more lovely and more temperate:
Rough winds do shake the darling buds of May,
And summer's lease hath all too short a date.
Sometimes too hot the eye of heaven shines,
And often is his gold complexion dimm'd;
And every fair from fair sometimes declines,
By chance, or nature's changing course untrimm'd;
But the eternal summer shall not fade,
Nor lose possession of that fair thou ow'st,
Nor shall death brag thou wander'st in his shade,
When eternal lines to time thou grow'st,
So long as men can breathe, or eyes can see,
So long lives this, and this gives life to thee.

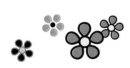

The Owl and the Pussycat

Edward Lear (1812–1888)

More like this

The Little Prince
Antoine de Saint-Exupéry

*Guess How Much I
Love You*
Sam McBratney

*The Complete Poems
of Winnie-the-Pooh*
AA Milne

The Owl and the Pussy-cat went to sea
In a beautiful pea-green boat,
They took some honey, and plenty of money,
Wrapped up in a five-pound note.
The Owl looked up to the stars above,
And sang to a small guitar,
'O lovely Pussy! O Pussy, my love,
What a beautiful Pussy you are,
You are,
You are!
What a beautiful Pussy you are!'

Pussy said to the Owl, 'You elegant fowl!
How charmingly sweet you sing!
O let us be married! too long we have tarried:
But what shall we do for a ring?'
They sailed away, for a year and a day,
To the land where the Bong-tree grows

And there in a wood a Piggy-wig stood
With a ring at the end of his nose,
His nose,
His nose,
With a ring at the end of his nose.

'Dear Pig, are you willing to sell for one shilling
Your ring?' Said the Piggy, 'I will.'
So they took it away, and were married next day
By the Turkey who lives on the hill.
They dined on mince, and slices of quince,
Which they ate with a runcible spoon;
And hand in hand, on the edge of the sand,
They danced by the light of the moon,
The moon,
The moon,
They danced by the light of the moon.

The Windhover

Gerard Manley Hopkins (1844–1889)

To Christ our Lord

I caught this morning morning's minion, king-
dom of daylight's dauphin, dapple-dawn-drawn Falcon,
   in his riding
Of the rolling level underneath him steady air, and striding
High there, how he rung upon the rein of a wimpling wing
In his ecstasy! then off, off forth on swing,
As a skate's heel sweeps smooth on a bow-bend: the hurl
   and gliding
Rebuffed the big wind. My heart in hiding
Stirred for a bird, – the achieve of, the mastery of the thing!

Brute beauty and valour and act, oh, air, pride, plume, here
Buckle! AND the fire that breaks from thee then, a billion
Times told lovelier, more dangerous, O my chevalier!

No wonder of it: sheer plod makes plough down sillion
Shine, and blue-bleak embers, ah my dear,
Fall, gall themselves, and gash gold-vermilion.

Sonnet 57
William Shakespeare (1564–1616)

Being your slave, what should I do but tend
Upon the hours and times of your desire?
I have no precious time at all to spend,
Nor services to do, till you require.
Nor dare I chide the world-without-end hour
Whilst I, my sovereign, watch the clock for you,
Nor think the bitterness of absence sour
When you have bid your servant once adieu;
Nor dare I question with my jealous thought
Where you may be, or your affairs suppose,
But, like a sad slave, stay and think of nought
Save, where you are how happy you make those.
So true a fool is love that in your will,
Though you do any thing, he thinks no ill.

Wedding Prayer
Robert Louis Stevenson (1850–1894)

Lord, behold our family here assembled.
We thank you for this place in which we dwell,
for the love that unites us,
for the peace accorded us this day,
for the hope with which we expect the morrow,
for the health, the work, the food,
and the bright skies that make our lives delightful;
for our friends in all parts of the earth.
Amen

The Passionate Shepherd to his Love

Christopher Marlowe (1564–1593)

Come live with me and be my Love,
And we will all the pleasures prove
That hills and valleys, dales and fields,
Or woods or steepy mountain.

There we will sit upon the rocks
And see the shepherds feed their flocks,
By shallow rivers, to whose falls
Melodious birds sing madrigals.

And I will make thee beds of roses
And a thousand fragrant posies,
A cap of flowers, and a kirtle
Embroider'd all with leaves of myrtle.

A gown made of the finest wool,
Which from our pretty lambs we pull,
Fair-linèd slippers for the cold,
With buckles of the purest gold.

A belt of straw and ivy buds
With coral clasps and amber studs:
And if these pleasures may thee move,
Come live with me and be my Love.

Putting it all together

On page 83 you will find four examples of ceremonies that combine Bible readings with poems or prose. They have been matched with music choices to give you some ideas of how the structure of the ceremony might look.

If you haven't thought about which readings you'd like at your wedding, a good starting point is to pick readings with a common theme or some link such as, love, companionship or respect. However, it's perfectly acceptable to just choose Bible readings and other passages which you particularly like or have some special meaning for you.

Suggested themes

Example 1
- Prelude: Sheep May Safely Graze
- Processional: Wedding March from *The Marriage of Figaro*
- Bible reading: For everything there is a season (see page 42)
- Second reading: Shall I compare thee to a summer's day? (see page 75)
- Recessional: Fanfare

Example 2
- Prelude: Nimrod
- Processional: Hallelujah Chorus
- Bible reading: Love (see page 32)
- Second reading: Never Marry but for Love (see page 58)
- Recessional: Wedding March

Example 3
- Prelude: Ave Verum Corpus
- Processional: Bridal Chorus from *Lohengrin*
- Bible reading: I am the vine and you are the branches (see page 34)
- Second reading: To My Dear and Loving Husband (see page 65)
- Recessional: Trumpet Voluntary

Example 4
- Prelude: Air from the *Water Music*
- Processional: Grand March from *Aida*
- Bible reading: Two are better than one (see page 43)
- Second reading: The Passionate Shepherd to his Love (see page 81)
- Recessional: Arrival of the Queen of Sheba

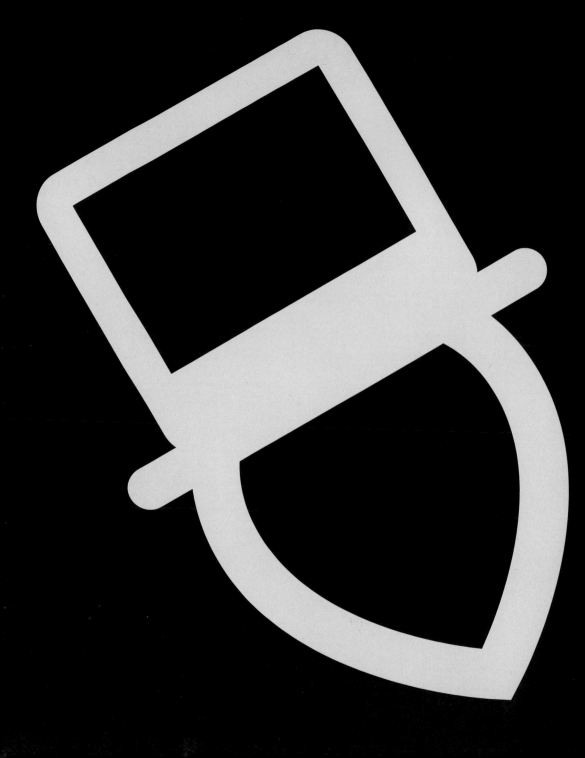

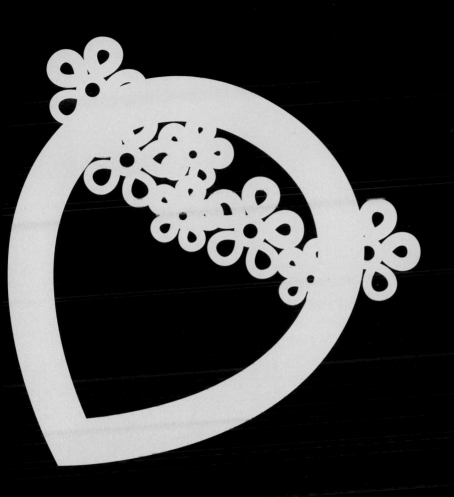

Civil
ceremonies

The structure of a civil ceremony

Nearly half of all weddings in the UK nowadays are solemnized in civil ceremonies.

As civil weddings don't have the elements of hymns and a sermon that Christian weddings include, readings tend to assume a great deal of importance on these occasions. That apart, the order of service is very similar to that of a church ceremony:

- Entrance music for bride
- Introduction
- Reading (optional)
- The marriage
- Reading (optional)
- Signing of the register
- Reading (optional)
- Exit music

At a register office wedding, you may decide not to have any readings, but you must obtain prior approval for any you do wish to use. Similarly, in weddings that take place in state-licensed venues, a registrar will need to approve your choice of readings. Remember, too, that civil weddings do not allow for any material with a religious content. Obviously this rules out biblical texts and hymns, but also more loosely spiritual material such as *The Prophet* or *Desiderata*.

If you want more freedom in the content of your ceremony, you might consider an alternative such as a humanist wedding. Here you'll have much greater flexibility to choose the readings you want, or – if you wish – you may even be able to write your own.

Generally, you are allowed to choose who delivers the readings on the day. This is often a useful way of including in your ceremony a close friend or relative whom you weren't able to choose as an usher or bridesmaid, or who lives too far away to be able to be more involved in the preparations.

Music and readings at a civil ceremony

As with a church wedding, music and readings can form an integral part of the civil ceremony. Although readings are optional many people include at least one, and often more. Bear in mind that your allotted time for the ceremony may have an impact on the readings you choose: three long pieces may not be practical. The same applies to music and it is best to discuss any ideas you have with the registrar before you become too attached to specific readings or pieces of music.

In a civil ceremony, the readings will take place before and after the marriage and you might also choose to have one after you have signed the register. Music and readings will add structure to the ceremony and give you the opportunity to make it more personal.

Civil partnerships

As civil partnership registration is a completely secular process, just like the civil marriage ceremony, you are prevented from having any religious service take place at the time of your registration.

A ceremony is not automatically provided when you register. Couples who wish to arrange for a ceremony at the time of registration should discuss this with the registrar when the initial arrangements are made. If you would like someone to give a reading you'll need to make sure it has no religious connotations as your ceremony has to be free of any mention of religion.

You will have the opportunity to say some words before you sign the registration schedule and you'll need to bring with you at least two other people as witnesses. If you did want to have a more spiritual ceremony, you could always arrange a separate humanist or other type of ceremony which would have special meaning to you.

Choosing non-religious readings

Once you've established how much scope your chosen ceremony allows, it's time to think about specific non-religious readings that you could include in your service. In theory, they could be any suitable extract from a work of literature, non-fiction or poetry. Here are a few pointers to get you started:

- Do you or your partner have a favourite poet, author or passage of writing that might be suitable?

- Look in books of quotations under headings such as 'love' and 'marriage'. Note any particular quotations or authors that you find appealing and look into them more closely. The Internet is a valuable tool for finding the author or full text of a piece you like.

- Keep your eye out for unusual sources. Children's books, for example, *Guess How Much I Love You* or extracts from *Winnie the Pooh*, are often good starting points. If you wish to reproduce your reading (for instance, in an order of service), you will need to make sure that it is out of copyright or that you obtain permission from the copyright holder, so bear this in mind while searching for your perfect piece.

- Try dipping into this book and reading out the most interesting bits to each other.

- Your register office may provide a booklet that contains a selection of readings approved for use in civil ceremonies.

- The British Humanist Association's guide to non-religious wedding ceremonies, *Sharing the Future*, has a chapter on readings with several interesting suggestions. Order through www.humanism.org.uk or call 020 7079 3580.

What are my options?

Suggested poems

A Red, Red Rose
(see page 105)

First Love
(see page 111)

She Walks in Beauty
(see page 106)

Doves poem
(see page 119)

As you will discover, the range of material available is enormous. The suggestions that follow include poetry, prose and texts from other traditions. What they have in common is a celebration of married life in all its fullness and variety. The best readings celebrate not just the first flash of passion, but all the enduring qualities of marriage, too: fidelity, companionship, mutual fulfilment, security and serenity.

Poetry and song lyrics

Poetry is a good option; its language well suited to the significance of the occasion. The more traditional might go for something from Shakespeare. Sonnet 116 ('Let me not to the marriage of true minds/Admit impediments...') is a popular choice, as are these lines from *Hamlet*:

Doubt thou the stars are fire;
Doubt that the sun doth move;
Doubt truth to be a liar;
But never doubt I love.

The 20th century has seen a multitude of poets and novelists writing on the age-old theme. TS Eliot, 'A Dedication to My Wife', WH Auden, 'O tell me the truth about love', and Adrian Henri's 'Without You' are popular. Another good choice is James Dillet Freeman's 'Blessing For A Marriage':

May you always need one another – not so much to fill your emptiness, as to help you to know your fullness...'

If you can get past his strange punctuation, e. e. cummings's 'I carry your heart with me (I carry it in/my heart)' is a stunning choice, and his *Selected Poems 1923–1958* is readily available. The images he uses in this poem are wonderful – there are no clichés and it's the perfect length for a reading. William Carlos Williams's 'The Ivy Crown' is just gorgeous, and is, again, a suitable length. His *Collected Poems* are also easy to get hold of.

Brian Patten's Love Poems is one of the most moving collections of the past few years. Have a look at Eithne Strong's 'Dedication' in the recent *Irish Love Poems*, which starts, 'To you/I have given./I want to be with you/along the way you have chosen.' This book is a real treasure trove of poems.

Or how about some song lyrics? These are becoming more and more popular with couples – it adds a twist to the more conventional reading and songwriters often manage to say things in truly original ways. Ozzy Ozbourne should be avoided perhaps, but have a look at Joni Mitchell's lyrics and poems for some ethereal stuff that encapsulates it all.

Prose

For great prose, try the ending of James Joyce's *Ulysses* for size. It's an incredible monologue and sums up all the passion, love and commitment in the world (and you don't have to plough through the whole book – it's in the last ten pages!). Here's a sample: 'I put my arms around him yes and drew him down to me so he could feel my breasts all perfume yes and his heart was going like mad and yes I said yes I will Yes.' However, it's an intrepid reader who will be willing to take this on and it probably isn't appropriate for the more conventional wedding venues.

There are also some wonderful older passages, such as Thomas à Kempis's 14th-century meditation ('Love feels no burden, thinks nothing of trouble, attempts what is above its strength, pleads no excuse of impossibility...'). Or for the more modern-minded, there are such gems as the famous extract from Albert Schweitzer's autobiography ('We must not try to force our way into the personality of another'), or the thoughts of Paul Kurtz: 'A successful marriage is one where each partner discovers that it is better to give love than to receive it.'

Suggested prose

Extract from *Les Miserables*
(see page 101)

Extract from Rainer Maria Rilke's Letters
(see page 114)

Love is a Great Thing
(see page 117)

Suggested texts from other traditions

Apache blessing
(see page 100)

Extract from a Native American wedding ceremony
(see page 103)

Eskimo love song
(see page 104)

A Chinese poem
(see page 104)

Texts from other traditions

Further afield, there are plenty of texts from other traditions that may suit. Kahlil Gibran's evocation of marriage in *The Prophet* is a very popular choice. But you'll also come across Eskimo love songs, African Bushman lyrics and Native American texts.

If you want a further selection beyond what you'll find here, try the anthologies. Among the best are *Love Poetry Across the Centuries*, and *A Book of Prayers for the First Years of Marriage*. You're guaranteed to find something to suit all tastes. Choose readings that show the many facets of love and marriage and make sure they convey what the day means to you.

Making a final decision

- Does the reading meet with approval from your registrar?
- Is the text really about marriage and not just about falling in love?
- Will it fit in with the rest of the order of service?
- Is it free of any material that might offend guests?

- Is it the right length? A reading that's too short may easily be drowned out by a coughing fit or crying baby, while a text that's too long may unbalance your whole ceremony.

- Will your chosen reader be comfortable with the words?

Music at a civil wedding

Choosing music for your wedding

Music will probably play an important part during your wedding ceremony. You can choose any music you like as long as it isn't religious. If you're not sure where to begin, start by narrowing it down to the style of music that you like and then thinking of pieces of music or songs within that genre that would be appropriate for a wedding. So, for example, if you particularly like classical, jazz or modern music, you might like your wedding ceremony to reflect this.

You certainly don't have to stick to classical music or traditional choices. Elvis fans might decide to play his songs; if you like tango, pick a selection of tango pieces. By keeping to the same style throughout the ceremony, you will also ensure it flows well. You obviously shouldn't choose anything that might cause offence to guests and it's good to remember that music sounds very different when you're listening to it at home by yourself and when it's played at increased volume to an audience.

The venue and the registrar might impose other limitations on the type of music you can have. For example, many registry offices won't allow musicians or live music, often because there just isn't enough space. You should always check early on, before you have booked anyone. You will find some suggestions for classical music on page 23 and any of the non-religious pieces would be suitable for a civil wedding. Below are some suggestions for more contemporary music.

Suggestions for contemporary music at a civil wedding

Entrance
- *Love me Tender* (Elvis Presley)
- *Can't Help Falling in Love* (Elvis Presley)
- *Perfect Day* (Lou Reed)
- *Every Breath you Take* (The Police)

Signing of register
- *When a Man Loves a Woman* (Percy Sledge)
- *Everything I Do* (Bryan Adams)

- *Crazy for You* (Madonna)
- *Have I told you Lately* (Van Morrison)
- *The Miracle of Love* (Eurythmics)

Departure of guests
- *Love and Marriage* (Frank Sinatra)
- *I Do, I Do, I Do* (Abba)
- *Walking on Sunshine* (Katrina and the Waves)
- *All you Need is Love* (Beatles)
- *That's Amore* (Dean Martin)

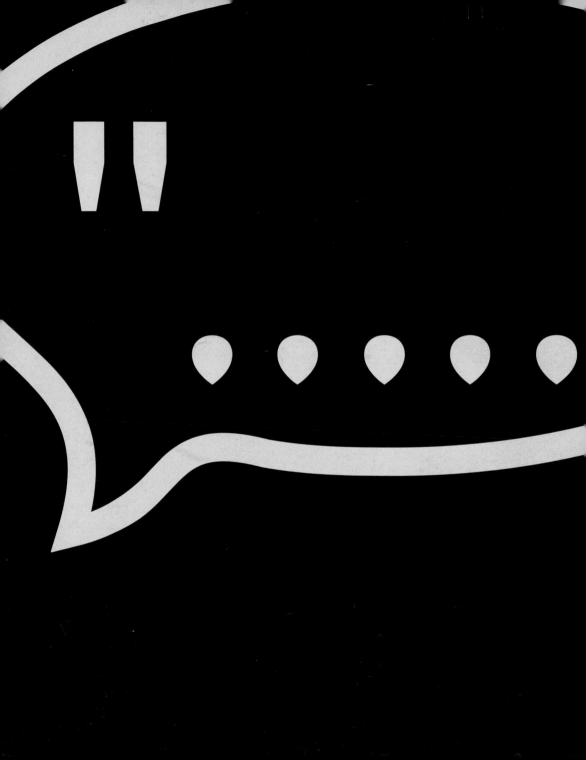

Readings

for a civil ceremony

Choosing your readings

The joy of love and marriage has been a focus of literature and narrative tradition since people started putting their thoughts and feelings into words. The passages of poetry and prose suggested in this book represent some of the best and most popular pieces written around the world over the last 800 years. While some are by such celebrated authors as Lord Byron and Wordsworth, many are traditional love poems that have been handed down for so many generations that their original author is not known.

When you have selected your ideal reading, check whether it is still in copyright. If it is, you cannot reproduce it (for instance, printed in an order of service) without first obtaining permission from the copyright holder (see pages 8–9).

On Your Wedding Day
Author unknown

Today is a day you will always remember
The greatest in anyone's life
You'll start off the day just two people in love
And end it as Husband and Wife

It's a brand new beginning, the start of a journey
With moments to cherish and treasure
And although there'll be times when you both disagree
These will surely be outweighed by pleasure

You'll have heard many words of advice in the past
When the secrets of marriage were spoken
But you know that the answers lie hidden inside
Where the bond of true love lies unbroken

So live happy for ever as lovers and friends
It's the dawn of a new life for you
As you stand there together with love in your eyes
From the moment you whisper 'I do'

And with luck, all your hopes, and your dreams can be real
May success find its way to your hearts
Tomorrow can bring you the greatest of joys
But today is the day it all starts.

Apache blessing
Author unknown

Winning combinations

Love Lives
John Clare
(see page 66)

Extract from *The Divine Comedy*
Dante
(see page 68)

Now you will feel no rain, for each of you will be shelter for each other. Now you will feel no cold, for each of you will be the warmth for the other. Now there is no more loneliness for you, for each of you will be companion to the other. Now you are two persons, but there is only one life before you. Go now to your dwelling place, to enter into the days of your life together. And may your days be good and long upon the earth.

Treat yourselves and each other with respect, and remind yourselves often of what brought you together. Give the highest priority to the tenderness, gentleness and kindness that your connection deserves. When frustration, difficulty and fear assail your relationship – as they threaten all relationships at one time or another – remember to focus on what is right between you, not only the part which seems wrong. In this way, you can ride out the storms when clouds hide the face of the sun in your lives – remembering that even if you lose sight of it for a moment, the sun is still there. And if each of you takes responsibility for the quality of your life together, it will be marked by abundance and delight.

Extract from *Les Miserables*

Victor Hugo (1802–1885)

You can give without loving, but you can never love without giving. The great acts of love are done by those who are habitually performing small acts of kindness. We pardon to the extent that we love. Love is knowing that even when you are alone, you will never be lonely again. And great happiness of life is the conviction that we are loved. Loved for ourselves. And even loved in spite of ourselves.

What is Love?
Author unknown

More like this

After The Lunch
Wendy Cope

Valentine
John Fuller

Oh Tell me the Truth
About Love
WH Auden

Sooner or later we begin to understand that love is more than verses on valentines and romance in the movies. We begin to know that love is here and now, real and true, the most important thing in our lives. For love is the creator of our favourite memories and the foundation of our fondest dreams. Love is a promise that is always kept, a fortune that can never be spent, a seed that can flourish in even the most unlikely of places. And this radiance that never fades, this mysterious and magical joy, is the greatest treasure of all – one known only by those who love.

Extract from a Native American Wedding Ceremony

Author unknown

May the sun bring you new happiness by day;
May the moon softly restore you by night;
May the rain wash away your worries
And the breeze blow new strength into your being,
And all the days of your life
May you walk gently through the world and know its beauty.

Tribal wish of the Iroquois Indian

Author unknown

May you have a safe tent
And no sorrow as you travel.
May happiness attend you in all your paths.
May you keep a heart like the morning,
And may you come slow to the four corners
Where man says goodnight.

Eskimo love song
Author unknown

You are my husband [wife]
My feet shall run because of you
My feet dance because of you
My heart shall beat because of you
My eyes see because of you
My mind thinks because of you
And I shall love because of you.

A Chinese poem
Author unknown

I want to be your friend for ever and ever
When the hills are all flat
and the rivers run dry
When the trees blossom in winter
and the snow falls in summer,
when heaven and earth mix —
not till then will I part from you.

A Red, Red Rose
Robert Burns (1759–1796)

O my Luve's like a red, red rose,
That's newly sprung in June;
O my Luve's like the melodie
That's sweetly play'd in tune.

As fair art thou, my bonnie lass,
So deep in luve am I;
And I will luve thee still, my Dear,
Till a' the seas gang dry.

Till a' the seas gang dry, my Dear,
And the rocks melt wi' the sun:
I will luve thee still, my Dear,
While the sands o' life shall run.

And fare thee weel, my only Luve,
And fare thee weel, a while!
And I will come again, my Luve,
Tho' it were ten thousand mile.

She Walks in Beauty

Lord Byron (1788–1824)

Winning combinations

These I can Promise
Mark Twain
(see page 116)

From Romeo and Juliet William
Shakespeare
(see pages 72–73)

She walks in beauty, like the night
Of cloudless climes and starry skies;
And all that's best of dark and bright
Meet in her aspect and her eyes:
Thus mellowed to that tender light
Which heaven to gaudy day denies.

One shade the more, one ray the less,
Had half impaired the nameless grace
Which waves in every raven tress,
Or softly lightens o'er her face;
Where thoughts serenely sweet express
How pure, how dear their dwelling-place.

And on that cheek, and o'er that brow,
So soft, so calm, yet eloquent,
The smiles that win, the tints that glow,
But tell of days in goodness spent,
A mind at peace with all below,
A heart whose love is innocent!

Extract from Song of the Open Road
Walt Whitman (1819–1892)

Listen! I will be honest with you,
I do not offer the old smooth prizes, but offer rough new
    prizes,
These are the days that must happen to you:
You shall not heap up what is call'd riches,
You shall scatter with lavish hand all that you earn or
    achieve.

However sweet these laid-up stores, however convenient this
    dwelling, we cannot remain there.
However shelter'd the port, and however calm the waters,
    we must not anchor here,
However welcome the hospitality that surrounds us we are
    permitted to receive it but a little while.

Afoot and light-hearted I take to the open road,
Healthy, free, the world before me,
The long brown path before me leading wherever I choose.

Camerado, I give you my hand!
I give you my love more precious than money,
I give you myself before preaching or law;
Will you give me yourself? Will you come travel with me?
Shall we stick by each other as long as we live?

A Good Wedding Cake

Author unknown

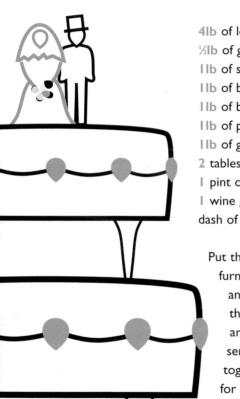

4lb of love
½lb of good looks
1lb of sweet temper
1lb of butter of youth
1lb of blindness of faults
1lb of pounded wit
1lb of good humour
2 tablespoons of sweet argument
1 pint of rippling laughter
1 wine glass of common sense
dash of modesty

Put the love, good looks and sweet temper into a well-furnished house. Beat the butter of youth to a cream, and mix well together with the blindness of faults. Stir the pounded wit and good humour into the sweet argument, then add the rippling laughter and common sense. Add a dash of modesty and work the whole together until everything is well mixed. Bake gently for ever.

The Day
Author unknown

May this be the start of a happy new life
that's full of special moments to share
May this be the first of your dreams come true
and of hope that will always be there...
May this be the start of a lifetime of trust
and of caring that's just now begun...

May today be a day that you'll always remember
the day when your hearts become one...

Wedding Day

Author unknown

Now comes the knitting, the tying, the entwining into one,
Mysterious involvement of two, whole separate people
Into something altogether strange and changing and lovely.
Nothing can ever be, we will never be the same again;
Not merged into each other irrevocably but rather
From now on we go the same way, in the same direction,
Agreeing not to leave each other lonely, or discouraged
    or behind,
I will do my best to keep my promises to you and keep
    you warm;
And we will make our wide bed beneath the bright and
    ragged quilt
Of all the yesterdays that make us who we are,
The strengths and frailties we bring to this marriage,
And we will be rich indeed.

First Love

John Clare (1793–1864)

I ne'er was struck before that hour
With love so sudden and so sweet,
Her face it bloomed like a sweet flower
And stole my heart away complete.
My face turned pale a deadly pale.
My legs refused to walk away,
And when she looked what could I ail?
My life and all seemed turned to clay.

And then my blood rushed to my face
And took my eyesight quite away,
The trees and bushes round the place
Seemed midnight at noonday.
I could not see a single thing
Words from my eyes did start –
They spoke as chords do from the string,
And blood burnt round my heart.

More like this

Astrophel and Stella IV
Sir Philip Sidney

Symptoms of Love
Robert Graves

Dea Ex Machina
John Updike

Married Love

Kuan Tao-Sheng (1263–1319)

You and I
Have so much love
That it
Burns like a fire,
In which we bake a lump of clay
Moulded into a figure of you
And a figure of me.
Then we take both of them,
And break them into pieces,
And mix the pieces with water,
And mould again a figure of you,
And a figure of me.
I am in your clay.
You are in my clay.
In life we share a single quilt.
In death we will share one bed.

A Birthday

Christina Rossetti (1830–1894)

My heart is like a singing bird
Whose nest is in a watered shoot;
My heart is like an apple tree
Whose boughs are bent with thickset fruit;
My heart is like a rainbow shell
That paddles in a halcyon sea;
My heart is gladder than all these
Because my love is come to me.

Raise me a dais of silk and down;
Hang it with vair and purple dyes;
Carve it in doves and pomegranates,
And peacocks with a hundred eyes;
Work it in gold and silver grapes,
In leaves and silver fleur-de-lys;
Because the birthday of my life
Is come, my love is come to me.

Winning combinations

My Delight and Thy Delight
Robert Bridges
(see page 71)

The Owl and the Pussycat
Edward Lear
(see pages 76–77)

Extract from Letters
Rainer Maria Rilke (1875–1926)

Marriage is in many ways a simplification of life, and it naturally combines the strengths and wills of two young people so that, together, they seem to reach farther into the future than they did before. Above all, marriage is a new task and a new seriousness – a new demand on the strength and generosity of each partner, and a great new danger for both.

The point of marriage is not to create a quick commonality by tearing down all boundaries; on the contrary, a good marriage is one in which each partner appoints the other to be the guardian of his solitude, and thus each shows the other the greatest possible trust. A merging of two people is an impossibility, and where it seems to exist, it is a hemming-in, a mutual consent that robs one party or both parties of their fullest freedom and development. But once the realization is accepted that even between the closest people infinite distances exist, a marvellous living side-by-side can grow up for them, if they succeed in loving the expanse between them, which gives them the possibility of always seeing each other as a whole and before an immense sky.

A Walled Garden
Author unknown

'Your marriage', he said, 'Should have within it
A secret and protected place, open to you alone.
Imagine it to be a walled garden.
Entered by a door to which only you have the key.
Within this garden you will cease to be a mother,
    father, employee,
Homemaker or any other roles which you fulfil in daily life.
Here you are yourselves, two people who love each other.
Here you can concentrate on one another's needs.
So take my hand and let us go back to our garden.
The time we spend together is not wasted but invested.
Invested in our future and the nurture of our love.'

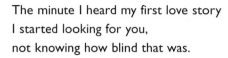
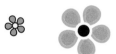

Untitled (1)
Rumi (1207–1273)

The minute I heard my first love story
I started looking for you,
not knowing how blind that was.

Lovers don't finally meet somewhere.
They're in each other all along.

These I can promise
Mark Twain (1835–1910)

I cannot promise you a life of sunshine;
I cannot promise riches, wealth or gold;
I cannot promise you an easy pathway
That leads away from change or growing old.

But I can promise all my heart's devotion
A smile to chase away your tears of sorrow;
A love that's ever true and ever growing;
A hand to hold in yours through each tomorrow.

Love is a Great Thing
Thomas à Kempis (1379–1471)

More like this

Valentine
Wendy Cope

Two Trees
Janet Miles

Scaffolding
Seamus Heaney

Love is a great thing, yea, a great and thorough good. By itself it makes that is heavy light; and it bears evenly all that is uneven.

It carries a burden which is no burden; it will not be kept back by anything low and mean; it desires to be free from all worldy affections, and not to be entangled by any outward prosperity, or by any adversity subdued.

Love feels no burden, thinks nothing of trouble, attempts what is above its strength, pleads no excuse of impossibility. It is therefore able to undertake all things, and it completes many things, and warrants them to take effect, where he who does not love would faint and lie down.

Though weary, it is not tired; though pressed it is not straitened; though alarmed, it is not confounded; but as a living flame it forces itself upwards and securely passes through all.

Love is active and sincere, courageous, patient, faithful, prudent and manly.

Untitled (2)
Author unknown

Treat yourselves and each other with respect, and remind yourselves often of what brought you together. Give the highest priority to the tenderness, gentleness and kindness that your connection deserves. When frustration, difficulty and fear assail your relationship – as they threaten all relationships at one time or another – remember to focus on what is right between you, not only the part which seems wrong. In this way, you can ride out the storms when clouds hide the face of the sun in your lives – remembering that even if you lose sight of it for a moment, the sun is still there. And if each of you takes responsibility for the quality of your life together, it will be marked by abundance and delight.

Doves poem

Author unknown

Two doves meeting in the sky
Two loves hand in hand, eye to eye
Two parts of a loving whole
Two hearts and a single soul
Two stars shining big and bright
Two fires bringing warmth and light
Two songs played in perfect tune
Two flowers growing into bloom
Two doves gliding in the air
Two loves free without a care
Two parts of a loving whole
Two hearts and a single soul
Two dreams found before too late
Two lives together bound by fate
Two people cling to one another
Two people in love with each other
Two doves, can you see them soar?
Two loves – who could ask for more?
Two parts of a loving whole
Two hearts and a single soul

Fidelity

DH Lawrence (1885–1930)

Fidelity and love are two different things, like a flower and
    a gem.
And love, like a flower, will fade, will change into something
    else
or it would not be flowery.

O flowers, they fade because they are moving swiftly; a little
    torrent of life
leaps up to the summit of the stem, gleams, turns over round
    the bend
of the parabola of curved flight,
sinks, and is gone, like a comet curving into the invisible.

O flowers, they are all the time travelling
like comets, and they come into our ken
for a day, for two days, and withdraw, slowly vanish again.

And we, we must take them on the wing, and let them go.
Embalmed flowers are not flowers, immortelles are not
    flowers;
flowers are just a motion, a swift motion, a coloured gesture;
that is their loveliness. And that is love.

But a gem is different. It lasts so much longer than we do
so much much much much longer
that it seems to last for ever.

Yet we know it is flowing away
as flowers are, and we are, only slower.
The wonderful slow flowing of the sapphire!

All flows, and every flow is related to every other flow.
Flowers and sapphires and us, diversely streaming.

In the old days, when sapphires were breathed upon and
   brought forth
During the wild orgasms of chaos
time was much slower, when the rocks came forth.
It took aeons to make a sapphire, aeons for it to pass away.

And a flower it takes a summer.

And man and woman are like the earth, that brings forth
   flowers
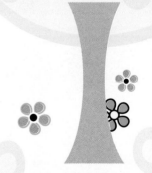
in summer, and love, but underneath is rock.
Older than flowers, older than ferns, older than
foraminiferae,
older than plasm altogether is the soul of a man underneath.
And when, throughout the wild orgasms of love
slowly a gem forms, in the ancient, once-more-molten rocks
of two human hearts, two ancient rocks, a man's heart and a
   woman's,
that is the crystal of peace, the slow hard jewel of trust,
the sapphire of fidelity.
The gem of mutual peace emerging from the wild chaos of
   love.

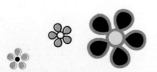

Putting it all together

You may both have certain readings or poems in mind and an idea of the kind of music you'd like to be played during your marriage ceremony, but often these ideas won't all work together. Whilst it's lovely to include aspects that have personal significance, or that you particularly like, it's also important to think about how everything will come together. You want the ceremony to flow smoothly, and mixing up classic and contemporary doesn't always work. Once you have discussed your ideas with the registrar, try playing the music and reading aloud your choices of poetry or other readings to see how it all sounds together.

Opposite are four examples of how some of the texts and music suggested in this book might be brought together for your ceremony, based on certain overall themes.

Suggested themes

Example 1: Classic

Traditional readings and classical music choices are combined here.

- Entrance music: Wedding March from *The Marriage of Figaro*
- First reading: She Walks in Beauty (see page 106)
- Second reading: Love is a Great Thing (see page 117)
- Exit music: Trumpet Voluntary (Jeremiah Clarke)

Example 2: The seasons

This ceremony takes nature as its starting point and it would suit a summer wedding.

- Entrance music: *Perfect Day*
- First reading: Extract from a *Native American Wedding Ceremony* (see page 103)
- Second reading: A Chinese poem (see page 104)
- Exit music: *Walking on Sunshine*

Example 3: Love

As love is the reason for marriage it seems obvious to celebrate it, but these songs and readings make it a focal point for the whole ceremony.

- Entrance music: *Sheep May Safely Graze*
- First reading: Extract from *Les Miserables* (see page 101)
- Second reading: A Red, Red Rose (see page 105)
- Exit music: March No 4 from *Pomp and Circumstance*

Example 4: Marriage

These readings talk of the actual institution of marriage as the bringing together of two people. The traditional music choices combine well with this theme.

- Entrance music: Grand March from *Aida*
- First reading: Extract from Rainer Maria Rilke's Letters (see page 114)
- Second reading: A Walled Garden (see page 115)
- Exit music: Wedding March (Mendelssohn)

At the
reception

Readings

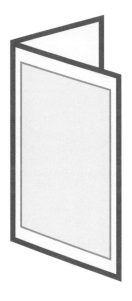

Most people concentrate on the readings at the actual ceremony and neglect to consider what they might like at the reception. While it's certainly more unusual to have readings at the reception, many people do choose to include them for a number of reasons. For example, if you had limited time at the ceremony venue, you may only have been able to have one or two readings; there might be other family members or friends who would like the opportunity to do a reading; or, due to number limitations, you might have guests who were invited just to the reception and you'd like to incorporate readings to make more of this part of your day. People also often include readings as part of their speech, as a way of expressing certain feelings. Over the following pages you'll find a selection of readings that are appropriate for the reception.

Music

Music at the reception is an important consideration and it will play a big part in the ambience of your wedding. The big event is the evening entertainment, but some couples also like to have background music playing as they arrive at the reception venue and greet their guests, or after dinner, as the main band are setting up.

No wedding is complete without guests, who are a little tipsy from champagne, taking to the floor and strutting their stuff. At most weddings there will probably be a huge age range amongst the guests and this can make the choice of music difficult – you don't want to exclude people from the dance floor by choosing music that half of them don't know or can't dance to. The key is to try and cater to everyone to a certain extent. If you have a live band or a DJ it's easy to cover different eras and genres of music so everyone has the opportunity to dance. However, if you'd like to do something a bit different, how about trying a jazz quartet, a swing band, a Gospel choir, a string quartet, an acoustic band or even a lone bagpiper?

Whatever you decide in terms of entertainment, you will need to ensure that they can play your choice of song for the first dance. It's the moment everyone is waiting for and, as well as being your first dance together as a married couple, it also signifies the start of the evening's entertainment and that it's time for everyone to really let their hair down.

20 Popular choices for the first dance

- *I Will Always Love You* (Whitney Houston or Dolly Parton versions)
- *Falling in Love* (Elvis Presley)
- *Wonderful Tonight* (Eric Clapton)
- *Fly Me to the Moon* (Frank Sinatra)
- *The Wind Beneath My Wings* (Bette Midler)
- *Have I Told You Lately* (Rod Stewart)
- *Don't Want to Miss a Thing* (Aerosmith)
- *My Heart Will Go On* (Celine Dion)
- *Three Times a Lady* (Lionel Richie)
- *I've got you Under my Skin* (Frank Sinatra)
- *What a Wonderful World* (Louis Armstrong)
- *Take my Breath Away* (Berlin)
- *Unchained Melody* (Righteous Brothers)
- *Nobody Does it Better* (Carly Simon)
- *It had to be You* (Harry Connick Jnr)
- *She's the One* (Robbie Williams)
- *Unforgettable* (Nat King Cole)
- *Groovy Kind of Love* (Phil Collins)
- *More than Words* (Extreme)
- *When a Man Loves a Woman* (Percy Sledge)

Suggested readings for the reception

From This Day Forward
Author unknown

From this day forward,
You shall not walk alone.
My heart will be your shelter,
And my arms will be your home.

This Day I Married my Best Friend
Author unknown

This day I married my best friend
...the one I laugh with as we share life's wondrous zest,
as we find new enjoyments and experience all that's best.
...the one I live for because the world seems brighter
as our happy times are better and our burdens feel
    much lighter.
...the one I love with every fibre of my soul.
We used to feel vaguely incomplete, now together we
    are whole.

Our Mother

Author unknown

You are the mother I received
The day I wed your son.
And I just want to thank you, Mum,
For all the things you've done.

You've given me a gracious man
With whom I share my life.
You are his loving mother and
I his lucky wife.

You used to pat his little head,
And now I hold his hand.
You raised in love a little boy
And gave to me a man.

A Valentine to my Wife

Eugene Field (1850–1895)

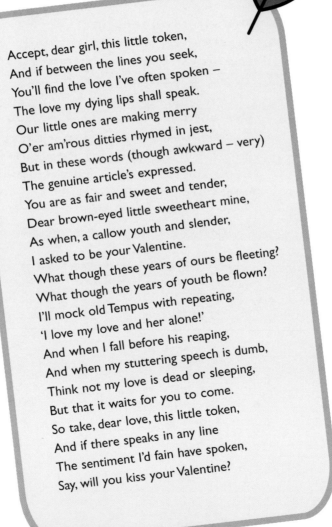

Accept, dear girl, this little token,
And if between the lines you seek,
You'll find the love I've often spoken –
The love my dying lips shall speak.
Our little ones are making merry
O'er am'rous ditties rhymed in jest,
But in these words (though awkward – very)
The genuine article's expressed.
You are as fair and sweet and tender,
Dear brown-eyed little sweetheart mine,
As when, a callow youth and slender,
I asked to be your Valentine.
What though these years of ours be fleeting?
What though the years of youth be flown?
I'll mock old Tempus with repeating,
'I love my love and her alone!'
And when I fall before his reaping,
And when my stuttering speech is dumb,
Think not my love is dead or sleeping,
But that it waits for you to come.
So take, dear love, this little token,
And if there speaks in any line
The sentiment I'd fain have spoken,
Say, will you kiss your Valentine?

My True Love Hath my Heart
Sir Philip Sidney (1554–1586)

My true love hath my heart, and I have his,
By just exchange one for another given:
I hold his dear, and mine he cannot miss,
There never was a better bargain driven:

My true love hath my heart, and I have his,
My heart in me keeps him and me in one,
My heart in him his thoughts and senses guide:
He loves my heart, for once it was his own,
I cherish his because in me it bides:

My true love hath my heart, and I have his.

Meeting at Night
Robert Browning (1812–1889)

The grey sea and the long black land,
And the yellow half-moon large and low;
And the startled little waves that leap
In fiery ringlets from their sleep,
As I gain the cover with pushing prow,
And quench its speed i' the slushy sand.

Then a mile of warm sea-scented beach;
Three fields to cross till a farm appears;
A tap at the pane, the quick sharp scratch
And blue spurt of a lighted match,
And a voice less loud, thro' its joys and fears,
Than the two hearts beating each to each!

The Miller's Daughter
Alfred, Lord Tennyson (1809–1892)

It Is the miller's daughter,
And she is grown so dear, so dear,
That I would be the jewel
That trembles in her ear:
For hid in ringlets day and night,
I'd touch her neck so warm and white.

And I would be the girdle
About her dainty dainty waist,
And her heart would beat against me,
In sorrow and in rest:
And I should know if it beat right,
I'd clasp it round so close and tight.

And I would be the necklace,
And all day long to fall and rise
Upon her balmy bosom,
With her laughter or her sighs,
And I would lie so light, so light,
I scarce should be unclasp'd at night.

Wedding
VOWS

Writing your own vows

If you are getting married by civil ceremony in the UK – for example, in a register office or an approved premises – then you may be allowed to include your own choice of vows in addition to the statutory words that legally bind you as husband and wife.

Although there is nothing in law to prevent you from including your own vows, some registrars have fixed views about what they will and will not permit. If your registrar will not allow you much freedom, you can ask to have another registrar appointed (from the same register office) who may be more flexible, but don't leave it till the last minute. In all cases, your registrar has the final say.

Personalized vows are a lovely way to inject personality and a unique flavour into a civil wedding ceremony. If one or both of you are getting married for the second time, writing your own vows will help to make the ceremony different and special to this new union.

All of the sample vows in this chapter can be adapted for a civil partnership.

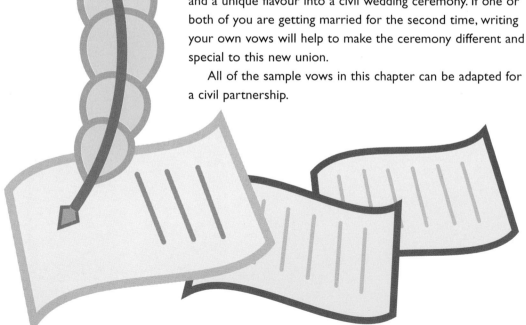

The statutory words

The minimum vows required for your marriage to be legal are as follows. These words must be said by both of you in your ceremony. You will usually be allowed to add your own choice of vows before or after the statutory ones.

In England and Wales the statutory declaration is:

I do solemnly declare that I know not of any lawful impediment why I, ____, may not be joined in matrimony to ____.

It is followed by these contracting words:

I call upon these persons here present to witness that I, ____, do take thee, ____, to be my lawful wedded husband/wife.

Legal alternatives

There are also two legal alternative declarations.

Declaration: *I know of no legal reason why I, ____, may not be joined in marriage to ____.*

Or by replying '*I am*' to the question: '*Are you, ____, free lawfully to marry ____?*'

These are followed by the contract:

I, ____, take you, ____ to be my wedded wife/husband.

or

I, ____ , take thee, ____ to be my wedded wife/husband.

In Scotland the couple say:

I solemnly declare that I know of no legal impediment why I, ____, may not be joined in matrimony to ____. I accept.

In Northern Ireland the statutory declaration is:

I know of no lawful impediment why I, ____, may not be joined in matrimony to, ____, to be my lawful wedded husband/wife.

A humanist ceremony

If you are looking for an even more personalized wedding ceremony in a civil venue or even in a beautiful garden or marquee, then think about a humanist wedding. This is a non-denominational celebration of a couple's love for each other and the bride and groom can write, or have influence over, every word of the ceremony. (You will also have to have a legally binding civil ceremony at the same time or earlier.)

An official humanist celebrant will provide you with some examples of a standard ceremony and help you to decide which elements you wish to include for your big day. You can then add or adapt words depending on what you want to say.

Suggestions for your vows

Non-religious options

I give you this ring as a symbol of our marriage and of my enduring love.

This ring symbolizes our relationship, which is whole and without end.

Our separate lives come together and are eternally one. The inside of this ring symbolizes our love for each other in our union, and the outside the world that we participate in as one.

Accepting and receiving the ring

I give you this ring as a symbol that part of me will for ever be a part of you.

I accept this ring as a symbol that part of you is for ever a part of me.

With this ring I give you my love as we journey through life together.

I accept this ring as a precious symbol of your love, which is always with me on our journey.

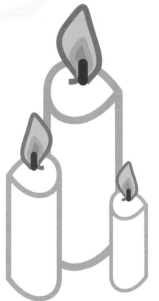

An alternative to rings

This candle is a token of our future life together, and the hopes and aspirations that we share.

The light of this candle burns as brightly as our future together and as strongly as our love for each other.

Renewing your vows

Vow renewal is gaining popularity in the UK. Although the various churches do offer vow renewal ceremonies, couples often take this opportunity to have a more flexible ceremony, including many personal aspects of their life together.

Points to remember when writing your vows

Do remember that, at the very heart of your vows, is the fact that this is a public declaration of your commitment to each other. The words should be created for others to witness and not simply as a private conversation between you and your partner. Don't embarrass your guests with over-intimate details or bore them with a lengthy monologue! The art is to express much in a few short, well-chosen statements.

Guidelines for writing your own vows

- Whether expressed in your own words or adapting existing ones, most vows follow a simple format: a declaration from each partner that he or she is willing and free to marry; and a commitment from each partner to love and care for each other whatever the future may bring.
- Include a promise to accept changes and a pledge to grow together during the experiences of a lifetime's partnership. Respecting your partner's right to grow and develop spiritually and mentally during the course of your relationship is a basic necessity for a happy marriage.
- Decide whether you each wish to write your own vows separately or whether you both wish to repeat the same vows.
- Consider whether you want to include responses from your guests after your vows, asking them to give their blessing to your marriage and to support your relationship in the future.
- When you have written your vows, discuss them with the celebrant who is to conduct your ceremony. He or she may have helpful suggestions to make or foresee potential problems. Remember that a professional such as a humanist celebrant is trained and experienced and will have a wealth of knowledge that can help you to create the perfect ceremony.
- Practise your vows with your partner or a trusted friend.
- Make a copy of your vows to have with you during the ceremony or repeat them after the celebrant. Nerves can play havoc with the memory and the last thing you want is to be worried about whether or not you will remember your words.
- Sincerity is the key to meaningful vows. Your words will have a profound effect on your guests. Even guests who are unsure of the wisdom of an alternative ceremony will not be able to find fault with vows that so obviously come from the heart.
- Finally, remember to speak slowly and clearly. You are asking your guests to witness your marriage and they need to hear your words.

Outlining your vows

The exercise below will help you to work out what you want to say in your vows. You and your partner should complete it separately. When you have written down all your ideas, swap papers and read through each other's. Make a note of your favourite bits of both, and use this as the basis for writing your vows together.

Write down the following:

- Ten words that describe your partner.
- Ten words that describe your relationship.
- A time when you both laughed so much that you cried.
- A time when you were unhappy and your partner was there for you.
- How you felt when you first realized you were in love with your partner.

- A short paragraph picturing your life together in 30 years' time.
- The names of any poems or readings you like, and what particularly appeals to you about them.
- Any song lyrics that reflect how you feel about your relationship.
- What marriage means to you.

- If relevant, what having a family means to you.
- Note down any 'themes' that recur. These may relate to a second marriage, getting married later in life, a particular event that has shaped your life together, or even your jobs.

Structuring your vows

When you have decided what to say in your vows, you need to structure them into an introduction, middle and end. Here are some examples.

Introduction

- I, ____ , take you ____ , for my lifelong husband/wife.
- I, ____ , take you ____ , as my partner on life's journey.
- I, ____ , take you ____ , to be my wife/husband, best friend, comforter and soulmate.
- I, ____ , choose you ____ , to be my partner for life.

Then follow with the main body of your vows.

Ending

- This is my solemn promise to you.
- I promise this to you today, tomorrow and for ever.
- I will share my life with you for as long as we both shall live.
- From this moment on, this is my true promise to you.
- Come what may, this shall remain my promise to you.

Seeking inspiration?

Look for inspiration from traditional vows that have stood the test of time. They contain moving and simple words that have forged marriages from generation to generation. They express in a nutshell the key promises upon which a happy marriage can be founded.

Jot down words and phrases from books, films or poetry that touch your heart and express your thoughts. Discuss the special moments in your relationships, whether happy, sad or humorous, to inspire personal meaning in the words you choose. The perfect vows demand the perfect vocabulary. Searching for words and phrases to match the depths of our emotions can be very frustrating. The following words and phrases will help you, but remember the final outcome has to come from the heart and from the bonds that exist between you and your partner.

Promises

To share the good and the bad parts of life together.
To love, honour, respect and cherish each other.
To respect each other's individuality.
To be kind, trusting, tolerant and understanding.
To be honest and faithful.
To stay together for life.
To bring happiness and laughter into the marriage.
To be a good friend.
To create a loving and stable relationship.

Personal attributes

Beauty, Candour, Charisma, Charm, Cheerfulness, Chivalry, Courage, Dependability, Determination, Elegance, Fidelity, Generosity, Gentleness, Grace, Honesty, Humility, Humour, Independence, Innocence, Integrity, Loyalty, Playfulness, Purity, Sense of Humour, Simplicity, Sincerity, Sweetness, Tenderness, Trust, Virtue, Worth

Personal descriptions

Ally, Angel, Beloved, Companion, Darling, Dearest, Friend, Goddess, Hero, Lover, Mate, Partner, Play-fellow, Soulmate, Sweetheart, Treasure

Adjectives

Absolute, Adorable, Alive, Amiable, Appealing, Ardent, Attractive, Beautiful, Binding, Blameless, Caring, Charming, Chivalrous, Complete, Considerate, Constant, Courageous, Cosy, Dauntless, Deserving, Desirable, Devoted, Ecstatic, Embracing, Emotional, Enduring, Energetic, Entire, Entrancing, Eternal, Excellent, Exciting, Fair, Faithful, Fervent, Forgiving, Formal, Gallant, Genuine, Good-humoured, Glorious, Growing, Happy, Hopeful, High-principled, High-spirited, Innocent, Jubilant, Lasting, Lively, Lovely, Loyal, Mutual, Noble, Popular, Praiseworthy, Precious, Predestined, Reliable, Romantic, Safe, Secluded, Seductive, Sensational, Sensual, Significant, Sincere, Snug, Soft, Solemn, Staunch, Stimulating, Sweet, Triumphant, Unconditional, Upright, Virtuous, Vivacious, Wonderful, Worthy

Verbs

Affirm, Appreciate, Aspire, Assert, Commit, Confide, Desire, Declare, Embrace, Endeavour, Entrust, Pledge, Proclaim, Promise, Protect, Reassure, Seek, Strive, Swear, Understand, Wonder

Negative words

Adversity, Anger, Desolation, Despair, Emptiness, Failure, Fears, Frailty, Jealousy, Neglect, Pressure, Poverty, Problems, Sickness, Sorrow, Suspicion, Weakness

Phrases

A measure of my love

A relationship built on love and honesty

A symbol of love

All the days of my life

As this ring surrounds your finger, so my love surrounds you

Bonds of love

Cherish, love and comfort

Companion in joy and comfort in adversity

Dearer than life itself

For an eternity of tomorrows

Friend, love and protector

From the depths of my heart

Give myself to you

Give you room to grow

Heart of my heart

I do not expect you to fulfil all my dreams, only to share
them and allow me to share yours

In sickness and in health

In sunshine and in shadow

In the presence of our friends and family I stand before you

Sample vows

Below are a selection of vows that would be appropriate for civil weddings, civil partnerships and humanist weddings. All of the vows can be adapted to suit your personal circumstances. Remember that you don't have to learn them by heart – you could write them on a card to read out or even have your registrar or celebrant read them for you to repeat.

'I, ___, take you, ___, to be my wife/husband. I will love you, comfort you, honour and protect you, and, forsaking all others, be faithful to you as long as we both shall live.'

'I, ___, take you, ___, to be my wife/husband. To have and to hold from this day forward, for better, for worse, for richer, for poorer, in sickness and in health, to love and to cherish till death do us part, and this is my solemn vow.'

'I will love you for the rest of our lives together. I promise to be a loving husband, a caring father and a supportive friend. Through times of sorrow and joy, poverty and wealth, I will cherish you and our family for as long as I live.'

'My love for you will never end. I will be there for you through good times and bad. I will give you the space you need to grow as an individual but be close enough to support you.'

Sample vows for a civil partnership

'I promise to love you and respect you. I will support you in difficult times and cherish the happy times that we will enjoy together.'

'I, ___, I vow to love, respect and honour you for the rest of my life. I will be faithful to you for as long as we both live. I will try to make you laugh when you are sad, have solutions for your problems, and provide comfort in times of trouble.'

Sample vows for a second marriage

If this is a second marriage for one or both partners, you will probably want to tailor your vows to reflect this. You might be at a slightly later stage in your life or maybe you have children from a previous marriage, in which case you might like to include them in the vows.

'I, ___, promise to be a faithful and loving companion to you, ___. I will endeavour to make you happy and content, to help you when you need help and to give you the space you need to be yourself. I welcome your family and friends into my life, and promise to build with you a stable family full of joy and laughter.'

'I, ___, solemnly swear to be a faithful and loving wife to you, ___. I welcome your family and friends into my life, and promise to make time for you and support you in everything that you do. I promise to help you make a strong family filled with love, respect and kindness.'

'I am here to express my love for you. I will make my life with you and I will welcome ___ and ___ as a part of our new family, loving and caring for them, as I will for you.'

Sample vows to involve guests

You might want to tell your guests before the ceremony that your vows will involve them.

Registrar: 'We have come here today to witness the commitment that ___ and ___ have made to each other. Do you, their family and friends, promise to offer them your support throughout their married life? To support their relationship and respect the promises they have made to each other?'

Guests: 'We do.'

Groom/Bride: 'I have made my vows to ___ and I would like to ask for the support of our family and friends. Will you stand by us in our married life, offering help and advice and showing commitment to our family?'

Guests: 'We will.'

Sample vows for those with children

If you have children, you will probably want to include them in your vows. This a really nice way of involving them and making it clear from the start that you are a family and your marriage ceremony is a way of making that official.

Groom/Bride: 'I am here today ___ to ask you to be my wife/husband. I ask you to love me and to share your life with me. I ask you to support me through everything we encounter in our married life. I ask you to embrace our new life as a family, with our children. Will you promise this?'

Bride/Groom: 'I will.'

Registrar: 'As ___ and ____ begin a new life together as a married couple, they also create a new family. Their children are part of this family and they would like to ask for a promise of commitment from their parents.'

Child(ren): 'We ask you to love us and support us as part of our new family. We ask for your protection and commitment to our development and happiness. Will you promise this?'

Groom and Bride: 'We will.'

Sample vows: question and answer format

Some couples choose wedding vows that follow a question and answer format. Here are some examples:

Registrar: '___ and ___, do you promise to share your life with each other, to be faithful to each other, honest to each other and to love one another through the good times and the difficult times?'

Bride and Groom: 'We do.'

Registrar: 'Will you offer each other your ongoing support in all your endeavours, encourage each other in all that you strive to achieve and work towards a solid relationship based on equality, honesty, love and respect.'

Bride and Groom: 'We will.'

Registrar: '___ ___, you have come here today to make a promise to share the rest of your life with ___ ___. Do you promise to love her, protect her, be faithful to her, and to offer her your support and commitment?'

Groom: 'I do.'

Registrar: '___ ___, you have come here today to make a promise to share the rest of your life with ___ ___. Do you promise to love him, protect him, be faithful to him, and to offer him your support and commitment?'

Bride: 'I do.'

Index of first lines

Index

Literary acknowledgements

Scripture quotations taken from the Holy Bible, New International Version. Copyright © 1973, 1978, 1984 by International Bible Society. Used by permission of Hodder & Stoughton Ltd., a member of the Hodder Headline Plc Group. All rights reserved.

Every effort has been made to trace copyright holders. We apologize for any unintentional omissions and would be pleased to insert an acknowledgement in subsequent editions.

About confetti.co.uk

Confetti.co.uk, founded in 1999, is the leading destination for brides- and grooms-to-be. Every month over 700,00 people visit www.confetti.co.uk to help them plan their weddings and special occasions. Here is a quick guide to our website

Weddings The wedding channel is packed full of advice and ideas to make your day more special and your planning less stressful. Our personalized planning tools will ensure you won't forget a thing.

Celebrations Checklists, advice and ideas for every party and celebration.

Fashion and beauty View hundreds of wedding, bridesmaid and party dresses and accessories. Get expert advice on how to look and feel good.

Travel Search for the most idyllic destinations for your honeymoon, wedding abroad or romantic breaks. Get fun ideas for hen and stag weekends.

Suppliers Thousands of suppliers to choose from including venues, gift lists companies, cake makers, florists and bridal retailers.

Café Talk to other brides and grooms and get ideas from our real life weddings section. Ask Aunt Betti, our agony aunt, for advice.

Shop All your wedding and party essentials in one place. The ranges include planning essentials, books and CDs, personalised stationery for weddings and celebrations, create your own trims, ribbons and papers, table decorations, party products including hen and stag, memories and gifts. If you'd like to do your shopping in person or view all the ranges before buying online, please visit the confetti stores.

Online
- Shop online 24 hours a day 7 days a week, use quick searches by department, product code or keyword, use the online order tracking facility and view brand new products as soon as they come out.

- Shop by phone on 0870 840 6060 Monday to Friday between 9 am and 5 pm.
- Shop by post by sending a completed order form to Confetti, Freepost NEA9292, Carr Lane, Low Moor, Bradford, BD12 0BR or fax on 01274 805 741.

By phone/freepost
Request your free copy of our catalogue online at www.confetti.co.uk or call 0870 840 6060

In store
London – 80 Tottenham Court Road, London, W1T 4TE
Leeds – The Light, The Headrow, Leeds, LS1 8TL
Birmingham – 43 Temple Street, Birmingham B2 5DP
Glasgow – 15–17 Queen Street, Glasgow, G1 3ED
Reading – 159 Friar Street, Reading, RG1 1HE

Executive Editor **Katy Denny**
Managing Editor **Clare Churly**
Executive Art Editor **Penny Stock**
Design **Cobalt id**
Production Manager **Ian Paton**